"The Object Lessons series achieves something very close to magic: the books take ordinary—even banal—objects and animate them with a rich history of invention, political struggle, science, and popular mythology. Filled with fascinating details and conveyed in sharp, accessible prose, the books make the everyday world come to life. Be warned: once you've read a few of these, you'll start walking around your house, picking up random objects, and musing aloud: 'I wonder what the story is behind this thing?'"

Steven Johnson, author of *Where Good Ideas Come From* and *How We Got to Now*

"Object Lessons describe themselves as 'short, beautiful books,' and to that, I'll say, amen. . . . If you read enough Object Lessons books, you'll fill your head with plenty of trivia to amaze and annoy your friends and loved ones—caution recommended on pontificating on the objects surrounding you. More importantly, though . . . they inspire us to take a second look at parts of the everyday that we've taken for granted. These are not so much lessons about the objects themselves, but opportunities for self-reflection and storytelling. They remind us that we are surrounded by a wondrous world, as long as we care to look."

John Warner, *The Chicago Tribune*

The joy of the series, of reading *Remote Control, Golf Ball, Driver's License, Drone, Silence, Glass, Refrigerator, Hotel,* and *Waste* . . . in quick succession, lies in encountering the various turns through which each of their authors has been put by his or her object. . . . The object predominates, sits squarely center stage, directs the action. The object decides the genre, the chronology, and the limits of the study. Accordingly, the author has to take her cue from the *thing* she chose or that chose her. The result is a wonderfully uneven series of books, each one a *thing* unto itself."

Julian Yates, *Los Angeles Review of Books*

The Object Lessons series has a beautifully simple premise. Each book or essay centers on a specific object. This can be mundane or unexpected, humorous or politically timely. Whatever the subject, these descriptions reveal the rich worlds hidden under the surface of things."

Christine Ro, *Book Riot*

. . . a sensibility somewhere between Roland Barthes and Wes Anderson."

Simon Reynolds, author of *Retromania: Pop Culture's Addiction to Its Own Past*

OBJECT LESSONS

A book series about the hidden lives of ordinary things.

Series Editors:

Ian Bogost and Christopher Schaberg

Advisory Board:

Sara Ahmed, Jane Bennett, Jeffrey Jerome Cohen, Johanna Drucker, Raiford Guins, Graham Harman, renée hoogland, Pam Houston, Eileen Joy, Douglas Kahn, Daniel Miller, Esther Milne, Timothy Morton, Kathleen Stewart, Nigel Thrift, Rob Walker, Michele White.

In association with

BOOKS IN THE SERIES

Remote Control by Caetlin Benson-Allott

Golf Ball by Harry Brown

Driver's License by Meredith Castile

Drone by Adam Rothstein

Silence by John Biguenet

Glass by John Garrison

Phone Booth by Ariana Kelly

Refrigerator by Jonathan Rees

Waste by Brian Thill

Hotel by Joanna Walsh

Hood by Alison Kinney

Dust by Michael Marder

Shipping Container by Craig Martin

Cigarette Lighter by Jack Pendarvis

Bookshelf by Lydia Pyne

Password by Martin Paul Eve

Questionnaire by Evan Kindley

Hair by Scott Lowe

Bread by Scott Cutler Shershow

Tree by Matthew Battles

Earth by Jeffrey Jerome Cohen and Linda T. Elkins-Tanton

Traffic by Paul Josephson

Egg by Nicole Walker

Sock by Kim Adrian

Eye Chart by William Germano

Whale Song by Margret Grebowicz

Tumor by Anna Leahy

Jet Lag by Christopher J. Lee

Shopping Mall by Matthew Newton

Personal Stereo by Rebecca Tuhus-Dubrow

Veil by Rafia Zakaria

Burger by Carol J. Adams

Luggage by Susan Harlan

Souvenir by Rolf Potts

Rust by Jean-Michel Rabaté

Doctor by Andrew Bomback

Fake by Kati Stevens

Blanket by Kara Thompson

High Heel by Summer Brennan

Pill by Robert Bennett

Potato by Rebecca Earle

Email by Randy Malamud

Hashtag by Elizabeth Losh

Magnet by Eva Barbarossa

Coffee by Dinah Lenney (forthcoming)

Compact Disc by Robert Barry (forthcoming)

Fog by Stephen Sparks (forthcoming)

Ocean by Steve Mentz (forthcoming)

Pixel by Ian Epstein (forthcoming)

Train by A. N. Devers (forthcoming)

magnet

EVA BARBAROSSA

BLOOMSBURY ACADEMIC

NEW YORK • LONDON • OXFORD • NEW DELHI • SYDNEY

BLOOMSBURY ACADEMIC
Bloomsbury Publishing Inc
1385 Broadway, New York, NY 10018, USA
50 Bedford Square, London, WC1B 3DP, UK

BLOOMSBURY, BLOOMSBURY ACADEMIC and the Diana logo are
trademarks of Bloomsbury Publishing Plc

First published in the United States of America 2020

Cover design: Alice Marwick

Bloomsbury Publishing Inc does not have any control over, or responsibility
for, any third-party websites referred to or in this book. All internet addresses
given in this book were correct at the time of going to press. The author and
publisher regret any inconvenience caused if addresses have changed or sites
have ceased to exist, but can accept no responsibility for any such changes.

Library of Congress Cataloging-in-Publication Data
Names: Barbarossa, Eva, author.
Title: Magnet / Eva Barbarossa.
Description: New York, NY : Bloomsbury Publishing, 2019. |
Series: Object lessons | Includes bibliographical references and index.
Identifiers: LCCN 2019008334 (print) | LCCN 2019016152 (ebook) |
ISBN 9781501348761 (ePub) | ISBN 9781501348778 (ePDF) |
ISBN 9781501348754 (pbk. : alk. paper) Subjects: LCSH: Magnets. |
Implements, utensils, etc. Classification: LCC QC757 (ebook) |
LCC QC757 .B37 2019 (print) | DDC 538–dc23
LC record available at https://lccn.loc.gov/2019008334

ISBN: PB: 978-1-5013-4875-4
ePDF: 978-1-5013-4877-8
eBook: 978-1-5013-4876-1

Series: Object Lessons

Typeset by Deanta Global Publishing Services, Chennai, India
Printed and bound in the United States of America

To find out more about our authors and books visit www.bloomsbury.com
and sign up for our newsletters.

CONTENTS

Prologue In which I eat hundreds of magnets xi

1 Birth In which humans find a stone with magical properties 1

2 Earth In which we discover we live on an ancient magnet 15

3 Home In which we use magnets to find our way 29

4 Alignment In which man and beast align to the magnetic fields 35

5 North In which we hunt for polar magnets 45

6 Health In which we believe magnets harm and heal 57

7 Transcendence In which magnetic fluids provide hope 67

8 Tricks In which we use magnets to make trouble 73

9 Toys In which we find magnets for play and pedagogy 81

10 Technology In which everything needs a magnet 91

Afterword In which I do not eat more magnets 99

Acknowledgments 105
Notes 107
Selected Sources 109
Index 111

PROLOGUE

Magnet, n. Something acted upon by magnetism.

Magnetism, n. Something acting upon a magnet.

—AMBROSE BIERCE, *THE DEVIL'S DICTIONARY*

Ambrose Bierce was a journalist, an author, and a Civil War veteran who wrote a column, starting in 1881, for the *Illustrated San Francisco Wasp*. These satirical definitions were eventually published as a book in 1906, which came to be known as *The Devil's Dictionary*. By then, Benjamin Franklin and his electrical experimentation was long dead, Europe was leading the pack on the study of electricity and magnetism, and the Magnetic Crusade of the British had instigated a race for Polar North. The nineteenth century was a period in time when science was popular, when the newspapers wrote of Charles Darwin, Pierre and Marie Curie, and Albert Einstein, and citizens thronged to lectures at the major science and exploratory institutions. It wasn't long before Bierce wrote his definitions that James Clerk Maxwell published his famous treatise *Equations* that redefined magnetism. These were mathematical equations confirming the theories of the great magnetic scientists— Michael Faraday, Carl Friedrich Gauss, and André-Marie Ampère—and, for scientists at least, they changed the world. When Maxwell's work was published, Einstein noted that reality has been peeled apart and what we see is not what is real. As time moves forward, the phenomenological world, the mechanical world, and the quantum world are peeling further and further apart and we are left, perhaps, with only the pleasure of the world we experience. To us, however, a magnet is a simple object we use, or more likely, something we are blissfully unaware of the integral part it plays in most of our technology.

When I was still quite young, five or six, our refrigerator had magnetic letters, each held to the refrigerator by three small magnets—except for the "I" which had space for only two. I would sit on the yellow linoleum floor and move them around, making shapes and words. I liked the letters, their bright colors, and the way they clicked to the refrigerator when you got them close enough.

But what I really liked were the magnets. They were small and rectangular. The lightly ribbed edges had a variable wale. They were slightly soft outside with a solid interior and if no one was looking—and they rarely were—I'd pry one out and pop it into my mouth. I wasn't in a hurry. I'd gnaw on it for hours until I'd eventually chewed off the soft outer coating. The plasticine taste would fade away, leaving only the iron. I would suck at the hard, inner core for hours, turning it around with my tongue, the slight metallic taste of the interior a bit tangy and utterly pleasing. I'd tuck it into my cheek and savor it until late in the day, then swallow the magnet just before we sat down to family dinner.

Refrigerator alphabets are not held up by particularly strong magnets. When I would take one from a letter it would slide down, a little less to hold it back from gravity. To avoid being caught, I took only one magnet from each letter at a time. The alphabet as a whole would slowly slip toward Earth as the force of its magnetic attraction weakened.

As a child I expected this to raise suspicions, as though it was obvious someone was stealing all the magnets. Even as a child I knew there was something aberrant about eating magnets. I was cautious. I stole when no one was looking. I mixed up the placement of the letters on the face of the refrigerator so there was no pattern in the absence.

When I ate the final magnet from a letter, I would put the letter in my pocket and take it out to be buried in a small sandpit in the forest behind the house. The disappearing letters would be noted, questioned, but in a rhetorical way. Curiosity for where they went, but never any suspicion or blame. In the world of adults, letters just got lost. And thus it went, for years. I ate hundreds of magnets. Alphabets were replaced. And then one day it stopped, and that was that.

Except perhaps it wasn't. In my teen years I had several close encounters with lightning. I fried car starters and microwaves, I was forbidden from using copy machines, my watches broke, and sometimes electricity would shoot out at me from light switches or the sockets. In college I broke computers and fax machines. Light bulbs flickered and died. Hand me a compass and it will misalign, spinning about, or simply dropping and end and stopping.

In this era of smart phones, mine has a tendency to lose its mind. The blue dot of the GPS rarely knows where I am. The optimal directions start somewhere I am not and take me to someplace I didn't ask to go. Sometimes it suggests I travel in circles, and it apparently thinks I can both walk on water and through solid buildings.

The more technology we have in the world, the more my troubles increase. MRI machines, magnetic hotel locks, the list goes on and on. I've spent a lot of time watching confused technicians try to repair things they've never seen. I've never explained about the magnets, even though I have always wondered if they were the cause. Last year the lock to a hotel room I was staying in demagnetized. Not the cards, but the lock itself. The hotel employees were so surprised they called others to see, while I sat and waited for them to find a way to get access to the room. It was an old building, and eventually someone dug around in a cupboard and produced an old key, round end, single tooth, and they opened the room, still marvelling at such an odd and spontaneous occurrence.

I've asked doctors and scientists what eating magnets does to one's body, if it could change the electrical field. Usually they stare while I explain what I ate, and then tell me that this is impossible, but I am unsure if the mean the magnet-eating, or the possibility that this could be a cause of anything.

Could a small but steady magnetic field from within change the way magnets and electricity interact with me? I've never found an answer. I am still curious. Along the way, I've learned a lot about humans and magnets, magnetism and hubris, and the ways the magnet tugs at our hearts, as well as created our world, man-made and before.

Humans have always been curious about the magnet. It has driven us to write, explore, mythologize, define and redefine the stone and its behaviors. The discoveries have been both complicated and humorous at turns, and today, perhaps so taken for granted we don't think twice about. The history of the magnet is, in a way, a history of anomalies. Things rarely stay the same, it is impossible to predict the magnetic behaviors of our world. Like weather, we may have an idea, and we recognize magnetism and magnetic effects when we see them, but we don't really know very much, and what has been true at one time, has been untrue at another, reversing, modifying, and moving, much like, we shall see, the magnet itself.

(No Model.) 4 Sheets—Sheet 4.

N. TESLA.

ELECTRO MAGNETIC MOTOR.

No. 381,968. Patented May 1, 1888.

Fig: 17.
Fig: 18.
Fig: 19
M
R
G
D
F
V
N
S
A
w
a
a'
b
b'

WITNESSES:

Frank E. Hartley.

Frank B. Murphy.

INVENTOR:

Nikola Tesla,

BY

Duncan, Curtis & Page

ATTORNEYS.

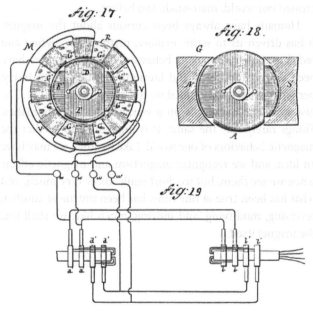

1 BIRTH

The history of the magnet begins 13.7 billion years ago with a *very* big bang; 9.2 billion years later gravity compels the dust clouds of our universe to coalesce into planetary forms, and the Earth is born. She is magnetic from the start, and soon after acquires magnetic shields to protect the surface from what blows in from space. Some of the oldest terrestrial rocks we know are a metamorphic gneiss from billions of years ago, rock striated with magnetic materials. We know two things for sure: that magnetic rocks exist around the planet, and that the magnet came into existence before humans.

The Earth took its time becoming this planet we recognize, from the geologic formations, to fauna and flora and other life-forms. The fossil record shows our first human ancestors were alive around 66 million years ago. This means that for the first four billion or so years, we were not here. It wasn't until two hundred thousand years ago that we might begin to recognize ourselves in our ancient ancestors.

Did the first humans find magnets and experience awe and fascination? Did they create stories to explain how this magic stone came to be and how it got its unusual powers?

We can't know. We must wait nearly all of those two hundred thousand years for the stories to be written. Language existed long before writing, but no ghostly whispers remain for us to hear. The first scripts are seven thousand years old, and we cannot decipher most of them. The oldest of these are found across the world in the form of fragments of wood and stone, beautiful glyphs and pictograms whose meaning we can only guess at. They seem to have lineages and elements from the natural world, but we don't know if one of them might have been a symbol for a magnet. However, from Easter Island to the Indus Valley to the Vinča culture of the Danube and on to China we have written records, a start on the path to finding the magnet.

The first written languages are from Egypt and Sumer. Around 3200 BCE people began to keep records: tax rolls, levies, the census. Civilization and cultures continued to grow, and with them, an expansion of written languages. By the twelfth century BCE we find Chinese, Persian, Sanskrit and Arabic documentation, and soon after, writings in ancient Greek and Old English.

The first written story that we have is the *Epic of Gilgamesh*. It was written down in Akkadian in the second millennium BCE. It is the story of the king of Uruk, an epic tale of the hero and his trials and tribulations. I like to imagine that Gilgamesh had a magnet to aid in his journey to the legendary Cedar Forest, but it isn't mentioned in the translations. The first mention of the magnet in literature comes from Homer, in the eighth century BCE. As with all early written myths, these are believed to be oral tales long told before they were finally written. We can assume the magnet was known and its behaviors noted, long before Homer wrote of it.

Tracing the ancient history of human interaction with the magnet takes us along two paths. First, the word; the name of the stone itself and its variation across time and language, which makes it difficult to track. And second, the artifacts of unwritten knowledge; the integration of the magnet into the creation of art and architecture, where it is clear the stone's properties were understood.

In English, the magnet was first called lodestone: lode, meaning "way," described the properties of the stone. It was similar to the lode star, which was the pole star, the star that showed the way. Forms of the word *magnet* are found in English from the fifteenth century onward. The *Oxford English Dictionary*'s first entry for the word *magnet* is from Philemon Holland's 1601 translation of Pliny. The etymology shows trails back to Greek (*magnes*), Latin (*magnetum*), and Old French (*magnete*) and thus into Old English. The word existed in its various forms for hundreds of years before settling into the spelling we are familiar with. From ancient times, writings suggest that its properties were known, in lapidaries and in metaphor.

The earliest source of our English word is from the ancient Greek, and there is more than one story about how the Greeks came to use the word *magnes* to describe this stone. The first is that the stone was named for a region where it was plentiful: Magnesia, in Lydia. The second, from the Greek poet Nicander, tells the story of a shepherd named Magnes whose boots stuck nail to stone. Nicander's writings were lost, but Pliny retells his tale. Another thread in the story of the magnet. So many lost writings referred to by others, the originals long gone. Stories of stories told. In a third tale, Magnes was a king (for whom Magnesia was named), and the stone was named after him. This last tale was told by Hesiod and includes Apollo falling so in love with a boy that he refused to leave the house of Magnes, the attraction so strong he could not be dislodged. We find in ancient Greek the use of magnet, magnes, and magnes' stone, but the Greek tales of the stone don't always use a version of the word *magnet*. It is also called the Stone of Herakles, which originates from the center of his temple-cult on Samothrace, where the magnetically rich Mount Ida is located.

In most languages the stone is described by its properties. Just as it is "a stone that leads (lodestone)," it is also "a stone that attracts," "a stone that repels," "a stone that points south," or "a loving stone." And it isn't always a stone, at times it is also called metal or iron.

Defining the magnet by its properties can lead to confusion, particularly with amber. Amber is fossilized tree resin that looks like a yellowish stone. When rubbed it also attracts, in its case not metal, but straw and cloth. It was known and prized in ancient times. Thus, one also has to sort through the geography and the context whenever old writings speak of a stone that attracts. Where and what this stone is, and how it came to be understood, is strewn across centuries of uninterpreted stories.

On our second path, there is evidence that multiple cultures understood and used the lodestone in art and architecture long before it was written of. We find carvings and statues, buildings and cities, aligned in ways that are not happenstance. Not only do they align to the north–south axis of magnetism, they align to the axis as it was in a particular time period. Because the magnetic poles shift over time, magnetic north has not always been in the same place. We can track the history of alignment with the ancient records of the magnetic pole locations as documented in the Earth's geologic record.

Ancient cities, from South America to China, align to the magnetic north of their time. There are also individual buildings that may have been aligned to magnetic north, not celestial or solar phenomena, as well as sculptures and petroglyphs that use the magnetic fields within the stones as a part of the art itself. We have no written record by their creators of any of these, and most are reasonably new rediscoveries from the past one hundred years. Absent a written history, it seems, we did not think to look for how our ancestors used the lodestone to create their civilizations. We looked to the heavens for alignment, rather than to the Earth.

In the deserts of the American West there are swirly lined petroglyphs. They are beautiful and compelling, some appearing abstract, some seeming to depict fluids or rivers or fields. Some have form; spirals and flows coming out of the headlike shapes of bipedal creatures. We do not know for sure what they mean, what stories they are meant to tell. Some anthropologists have suggested they are symbols of galaxies, or waves from the sky. Others suggest the shapes represent visual hallucinations produced by plants such as jimsonweed, each plant having a particular incarnation in the mind's eye, from swirls to triangles. Still others propose they are maps or wayfinding rocks, to peoples or water or villages. We may never know for certain the meanings of these symbols, but we do know that many align to the magnetic lines within the rocks.

These magnetic lines are not visible to the eye. They are part of the inner structure of the stones, likely caused when lightning hit these stones. A rock struck so maintains a magnetic field based on the path of the electricity. They show no visible or textural changes. The only way to know the path of the lightning, and the thus the shape of the magnetic field, is to run a lodestone close to the rock, to feel your way. The creators of the images must have stood close to these rocks, lodestone in hand, detecting their magnetic field lines before creating these images.

In southern Mexico and Guatemala statues called "fat boys"—enormous, corpulent carved images of people—are strewn about Olmec and Mayan ruins. Believed to have been carved between 1200 and 300 BCE, they stand nearly four feet tall, and are carved from single blocks of stone. Most of their belly buttons are magnetic. Some also have strongly magnetic right temples. There is no visible variation in the stone, no insertion of magnetic rock. The same ruins also house a few turtle sculptures, also fat, with magnetic beaks. In the twentieth century, scientists discovered that loggerhead turtles possess some of the most sophisticated magneto-navigation abilities of the animal kingdom. They align to the complexities of the magnetic fields in astonishing ways, possibly seeing these fields in four dimensions. Did ancient peoples not only harness the lodestone for their use, but also understand magnetoreception and that other species can see these fields that we cannot? We will never know.

We find written mention of the magnet by the sixth century BCE. The Chinese, Arabs, and the Greeks documented the natural world, including geography, geology, and astronomy, and the magnet is classified in these works. These early records are largely descriptive of the stone and its properties, not mechanical or utilitarian. The world is still attributed to creators and gods, the magic of creation went unquestioned, and this stone appeared to be magical.

Greek authors had many explanations for what they saw. Over a span of six hundred years, from 600 BCE to just after the turn of the millennium, opinions abounded. Thales of Miletus believed the magnetic stone had a soul. Theophrastus believed they came in male and female form, explaining the properties of attraction and repulsion. Pliny the Elder wrote of the "hatred and friendship of deaf and insensible things." Plutarch thought it could breathe, describing how it inhaled and exhaled to affect objects around it. Democritus thought the stone had sympathy, like attracting like, and Epicurus thought the magnet emanated atoms that caused a wind. It wasn't just explanations of the how the stone worked that they wrote of, but also what it could be used for. Galen proposed the stone had medicinal properties, and he was not the only one. Chinese, Japanese, and Vedic sources also found uses for the stone in healing.

Early Chinese writings are largely divinatory. Geomantic writings are found from the Shang Dynasty (1600–1050 BCE). It begins with plastromancy, divination by plastrons from the underside of a turtle. Upon these were etched symbols and together they created a vision of the cosmos. The luopan—a "feng shui compass"—was built upon this, another layer of meaning, another means of understanding. In China, the needle pointed south. It was added to the luopan in the fifth century BCE, used to align the known world and its objects to the cosmos. The *Guiguzi*, a later collection of writings from the fifth to third centuries BCE, describes the creation of other magnetic divination tools. One of the most interesting was called the south-pointing soup spoon. It is described as a soup ladle that would pivot and spin, with the handle pointing south.

Ptolemaic Egypt (300–35 BCE) created magnetic temples in which statues were said to have levitated. It is written that upon the death of his wife Arsinoe II (who was also his sister), Ptolemy II Philadelphus hired an architect to build a temple to demonstrate her ascension from human to god. Catasterism, whereby a hero or queen became a star upon dying, was not an unusual concept for Ptolemaic Egypt, or for Greece. Arsinoe was to become the pole star, when her ascension was complete. The architect (who had previously worked for Alexander the Great) designed a temple with a magnetite roof. When the iron-headed statue was put in place, she would levitate in the center, a sign to all who visited that she was indeed to be worshipped, that she was rising above us all, free, beyond. Perhaps for the best, both he and Ptolemy died before the temple was completed, as Earnshaw's theorem, in 1842, eventually proved that levitation with static magnets such as they were attempting would have been impossible.

The Sun Temple of Karnak (third to first millennium BCE) was said to hold a giant lodestone that kept the temple together, threw ships off course, and levitated statues. There are stories of crypts with altars that levitated, and of palaces and fortresses that used giant lodestones to keep those bearing arms from being able to enter. These tales come from Egypt and China and Wales and many places in between. These were historical accounts, not myths, written as fact.

The Aztecs created discs from magnetized volcanic glass. Referred to as mirrors, it is believed they were used for scrying and for seeing across time and space. John Dee, an astrologer and astronomer who acted as advisor to Queen Elizabeth I, possessed one that he reportedly used for divination, to communicate with angels.

Some early descriptions cross the lines between medicine and magic. The Daktyloi and their magnetic cult of navigators, stories of healing stones, scrying stones, and those that could be used for surgery. They are defined in usage for good, and for evil, aligning, perhaps, to the polarity of the stone itself. Some authors say the stone can be used to increase fertility, and some to block it. Centuries of variable recommendations lead us to the alchemists of the Middle Ages. For some, the stone was part of their kit in the hunt for the philosopher's stone.

It is with the compass, however, that we see, from a modern perspective, the first useful application of this magnetic stone. The Arabs are the first to write of it, in the eighth century, writing of the marine compass in treatises on navigation and sailing. The Chinese used the land compass for terrestrial navigation, traveling across deserts such as the Gobi, and later as they crossed the sea, as part of the extensive trade routes that ran from North Africa to China. By the thirteenth century even Europe is writing about the compass—they were late to the game—and the knowledge of its use seems spread across the seafaring world.

Knowledge of the compass, however, did not lead to precise navigation for hundreds of years. So many external elements can disturb the accuracy of the compass, from motion across land, the roll of the sea, to the swift elevation changes of air travel. The Earth itself is a complicated magnetic body and it took centuries to realize the troubles arose not only with the compass, but also with the Earth itself. The compass was used in conjunction with other tools, increasing accuracy across all, but none alone could help a navigator find his way.

The compass will not begin to be refined until much later, when the drive to harness terrestrial magnetism leads to an extensive plan of observations and experiments that aid in the creation of maps that enhance compass usage.

Soon after the magnet appears in descriptive passages, we find magnetic metaphors. In the fourth century BCE, in Plato's *Ion*, Socrates says, "The gift which you possess of speaking excellently about Homer is not an art, but, as I was just saying, an inspiration; there is a divinity moving you, like that contained in the stone which Euripides calls a magnet, but which is commonly known as the stone of Heracles."

In the third century, Claudian of Alexandria wrote some nicely spicy poetry about magnetic attraction. In *The Magnet* he writes a "tale of two statues, Mars of iron and Venus of the loadstone. The stone sighs and burns, and smitten with love recognizes in the iron the object of its desire, while the iron experiences a gentle attraction for the stone." With a slight nudge the statues move across the gallery floor until CLICK they find themselves wrapped in each other's arms.

Today, we use the same metaphors that have been around for more than two thousand years: expressions such as "magnetic attraction," "opposites attract," "true north," and "moral compass" are part of our lexicon. Magnetism is an unnoticed part of who we are and how we understand the world.

The early writings described the stone in terms of its properties and suggested uses for magic, healing or wonder. It was eventually noticed that the stone, or a needle magnetized by the stone, aligns to the north and south. This consistent action becomes a tool for navigation but the inconsistency in its behaviors open bigger questions. What is this force? Why does it work? Why doesn't it always work? Why does it vary? Inconsistencies lead to curiosity; what do we know? Let us start the exploration with the Earth herself.

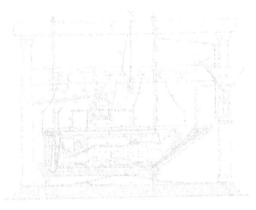

J. Young,
Electro-Magnetic Bathing Apparatus.

Nº 32,332.

Patented May 14, 1861.

Fig. 1

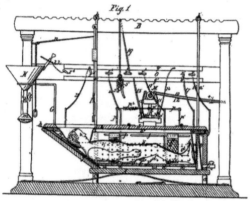

Fig. 2

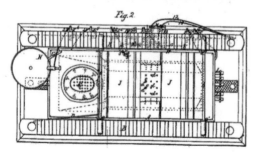

Witnesses

Inventor

James Young

2 EARTH

Terrestrial magnetism is an inconsistent force. The simplicity of a magnet in our everyday lives—bar magnets clacking together or hanging a photo on the fridge—is anything but simple at the planetary level. There is a magnetic field that migrates, a force that wavers, and poles that wobble and move. And that is just the beginning. These have both diurnal and secular changes, daily and over the long term. The magnetic force varies in strength over the day. The magnetism we encounter on this Earth is not the only force we must contend with, however. There are extraterrestrial forces as well. We exist within a magnetic universe contributing its own forces, and with the winds and weather of magnetic storms. The magnetic fields vary by body: the Sun, Mercury, each have different fields and different effects upon our world. It has taken us millennia to understand these exist, and there is still much we do not know.

In the ancient world, it was the philosophers who first described the magnet. Theirs was the observation of the natural world by the eye and by the senses, without experimentation and without tools to observe beyond the naked eye. Lucretius wrote *De rerum natura* (*The Nature of Things*) to describe matter, space, and the atoms, as he envisioned them. Strabo wrote the *Geographica*, a descriptive history of places and peoples. Pliny the Elder wrote *Naturalis historia*, an encyclopedic (for the time) history of the natural world including geology and mineralogy. Magnets were part of what each observed and catalogued in these works.

In those days, the Earth was still the center of the universe, the continents were fixed in place, and other than the sinking of Atlantis, it would be long before anyone would believe that there were moveable plates that could shift across the surface of the planet. Heliocentrism was centuries away. To wit, the Earth came into existence exactly as it was experienced, unquestioned in its perfection. It had yet to be conceived as changeable, or fluid; its origins went unquestioned. It simply was. Theories and opinions as to what things were and why were numerous, but there was no way to know, there was not yet a science to experiment or to prove. These were empirical times: what is my experience of this magnetic stone, how do I see it, what can I do with it?

In the beginning, we knew that magnetic stones attracted and repulsed each other, as well as attracted certain metals. The stone had properties that could be known and described. The discovery of a magnetized needle, a free-floating magnetic needle suspended from a silken cord, exposed a new unknown. Something turned this needle northward. This was something new, and it needed an explanation.

As usual, there were many theories; it was thought, perhaps, to be due to a large magnet pulling all the needles toward the north. Or perhaps something, as yet undefined, off the planet pulled the needles. Or perhaps it was a large magnetic island in the north, or the pole star itself. Whatever the cause, it was a *fait accompli*. The needle turned north, there was no changing this. (Or south, if one was Chinese.) Those who wrote of this phenomenon were free to choose their own explanations, as were the cartographers, who included magnetic islands on their maps. Olaus Magnus included magnetic islands on his maps. Gerardus Mercator put a giant black rock, which he called the Rupes Nigra, in the center of the Arctic on his 1569 world map. Much as there were dragons inhabiting unknown spaces, hunks of magnetic rock now dotted the north, explaining the mystery of the compass.

The harnessing of the magnet into the magnetic compass marked a significant leap, not only as a tool for navigation but as a way of seeing the world anew. Now one could know the direction of travel night and day, regardless of whether the pole star was visible, or the weather was bad. But what to do about the anomalies and the inconsistencies? The compass was a new kind of magic. It allowed sailors to travel further from the coasts and enabled safer crossings of land. It wasn't perfect, and it wasn't the only tool used for navigation. To work well, particularly at sea, it had to be used in conjunction with a second measuring device, be it the stars or a sextant, or an experienced navigator's knowledge.

People began using compasses at least as early as the eighth century—which is when we first have sophisticated writings about it—a thousand years before John Harrison's marine chronometer solved the longitude problem.

Early users recognized that the compass readings varied, but didn't understand why. Even now, sea charts have "magnetic anomaly" written on them where things go awry. No explanation offered, just a warning that the compass won't read true. As the centuries ticked on and as recorded observations of the magnetic behaviors of the planet grew in detail across the globe, the behaviors of the magnetic fields turned out to be even odder than anyone predicted. Observations, which people had assumed were fixed to time and place, varied within the day, across days. Even the fields themselves seemed to move. This variability complicated seafaring and commerce. And as the world began to shrink during the Age of Exploration, with ships remaining longer and longer at sea, people began to ask why, in the interest of creating a model of how terrestrial magnetism works, to better predict and harness it. To turn the Earth itself to their advantage.

In the late sixteenth century, Queen Elizabeth asked her personal physician, the scientist William Gilbert, to investigate the western drift of the compass. Sir Francis Drake had just returned from a significant voyage across the Atlantic, during which Drake's crew kept detailed observations of the compass's unexpected behaviors. When they had traveled far enough west, his compass began to point to the east, toward magnetic north. We know now that this is declination, that magnetic north and true north are not the same. Declination is the variance between magnetic north and global north. Because magnetic north moves, if one does not know the position of magnetic north relative to global north, one cannot get a true reading from a compass. Variation over time without maps or secondary ways of aligning could result in shipwreck or being lost at sea.

Declination wasn't the only strange reading Gilbert had to contend with, however. Magnetic inclination is the strength by which a needle is pulled toward the Earth, because the magnetic field is not parallel to the surface. Georg Hartmann discovered inclination (now called dip) in 1544, which noted how terrestrial magnetism pulled the needle down toward the Earth with varying strength, but it was the sailors who realized this changed depending on where one was. In 1581, Robert Norman discovered a way to measure inclination. Inclination would later go on to cause trouble for airplanes and submarines down the line, but in the sixteenth century, it was merely one more strange behavior of a needle.

Gilbert was the sort of scientist who performed his experiments in his laboratory. To investigate terrestrial magnetism, he created small magnetized spheres to represent the Earth. Gilbert referred to these as his "earthkins." They included a metal core surrounded by a brass casing. Both parts were etched with lines of longitude and latitude, among other symbols. Gilbert would run a magnetized needle along the earthkin and observe the ways in which the needle bent toward the globe as well as the poles. He concluded that to explain the action of the needle against the sphere, the Earth itself must be a magnet. He published his findings in 1600, in *De magnete*. He included a survey of the known history of magnetism, and an explanation of the terrestrial phenomena with numerous illustrations

Gilbert envisioned the planet as having a giant bar magnet stuck in the middle. The strongest forces of a bar magnet are at its poles, which explained both the pull to the poles and the declination around the equator, but not the localized anomalies or secular and diurnal shifts that sailors and magnetic observers noted on their voyages. While he doesn't explicitly say so in his book, Gilbert's model of the Earth's magnetism required a heliocentric model. (His reticence on this point may have had something to do with the fact that the Catholic Church had just burned Giordano Bruno at the stake in Rome for expressing such a belief.) While Gilbert wasn't entirely correct about the makeup of the interior or the mechanism, his recognition of the Earth's magnetism started others down the path of exploration and inquiry.

Gilbert failed because his conceptualization was too simple. Rather than a bar magnet stuck in the middle, today we know the Earth's interior contains an ocean of liquid metal, a body of liquid larger than any surface ocean, with what amounts to its own weather system. The (mostly) iron body is not fluid in the way we imagine: it is thick like mercury but has a viscosity similar to water. The heat and the pressure make it so. Think of it this way: this is the largest ocean on Earth and like those on the surface, it has daily tides, the diurnal variation that we see in our surface oceans over the course of the day. And also like these, the moon and other extraterrestrial bodies can cause variations.

In 1937 the Danish geophysicist Inge Lehmann realized that the refraction of the seismic waves passing through the Earth did not align with a model of a liquid core. She created a new model wherein our liquid iron sea enwraps a solid iron core. The mantle surrounds these cores, and around all of this, sitting atop the mantle, is the crust. The crust and the upper mantle are the rigid crust of the Earth upon which we live.

In the 1960s it was discovered that the uppermost part of the mantle was not one solid block of unmovable material, but rather has a slowly elastic behavior over very long timescales. The crust and this elastic layer form interlocking tectonic plates, which can slide, crashing together, or separate, changing the shape of our continents, creating new islands, or opening rifts.

The current prevailing theory for the existence of the magnetic field is that the Earth is a geodynamo. Joseph Larmor, an Irish physicist and mathematician, first proposed this theory in 1919 but, again, it took another fifty years for scientists to accept the theory. A geodynamo is a convective dynamo; this means that the rotating and convecting fluid in the core of the Earth is electrically conductive. The planetary rotation keeps this fluid churning and in motion, which in turn generates electricity, which creates and supports the magnetic field. This requires mass, movement, heat, and rotation. If something goes awry, the field could disappear. Without the field, we would lose our atmosphere. Mars once had a magnetic field, which we know due to the presence of magnetic rocks on its surface. There are many theories as to why it—and the atmosphere—disappeared, but the end result was a barren planet.

Due to its rotation, the Earth is subject to Coriolis effects, which create the currents at sea and also in the molten core. At the surface level, this helps us understand the dynamics of the oceans and the currents and is of great interest to meteorology. But it also acts upon our inner, molten sea. The inner, liquid core is not entirely liquid; there are occasional chunks of material shifting in the churning sea, and nonstandard patterns emerge. It is all far more complicated than this. It is, however, the geodynamo and the Coriolis effect that create the western drift that caused problems for navigators in the Middle Ages, even though they did not know the source. Back on the surface, deposits of iron or magnetic stone in the sea or on shores can also cause anomalies in the behavior of the compass. These are often called magnetic deviations, and as previously noted, on sea charts often appear as the nonspecific "magnetic anomaly."

By Gilbert's time, magnetism had taken hold of the scientists of Europe, and it wasn't soon to let go. Ships had started keeping records of observations when out to sea, but these observations were neither extensive nor systematic. Starting in 1698, Edmund Halley, of comet fame, embarked on two multiyear trips to take magnetic observations. He created magnetic charts showing igonic and isogonic lines. The trouble was, as always, the lines moved. Creating what seemed to be a definitive chart, for those who did not realize that was not possible, resulted in shipwrecks. Halley was trying to answer two questions: Could enough observations provide a means of establishing longitude? And could he take enough measurements to uncover regular laws of magnetism?

Centuries of observations on the surface mapped the behaviors and anomalies (which of course changed over time), but it wasn't until the twentieth century that a great deal of geophysical science came together to describe the internal actions of the planet and create a framework for understanding. However, while the framework can explain the big picture, we still cannot predict the magnetic weather that affects our planet. At its simplest, we now know the magnetic field varies in three ways. Inclination, or dip, is the strength of the pull of the needle toward Earth. Declination is the variances between the magnetic pole and the geographic pole. Force is the strength of the magnetic field. Each varies over the day, and over time, and they do not necessarily vary in unison.

We can track the history of the Earth's magnetic fields over time in cooled volcanic rock. When lava flows it acquires the magnetic record of the Earth's field at that particular time and place. When it cools, it keeps that memory, if you will. When you heat rock above the Curie temperature, it loses its memory and takes on the current field. Paleomagnetism is the study of the information stored in rocks and sediment, which provides a record of the past. In the early twentieth century, Bernard Brunhes, a French geophysicist, pioneered this work, based on discoveries made at an extinct volcano in the Auvergne region of France. He was the first to discover that the Earth's polarity had reversed. Like many of the magnetic discoveries, it took more than fifty years for this to be accepted as true.

Brunhes made his discovery in central France, in 1906, after realizing that some rocks were magnetized in the opposite direction to the current, local field. His research, and that of other scientists, eventually confirmed that the Earth's polarity has reversed several times—but not why, or what causes it to reverse. We do know the fields weaken before they flip, and that this results in the polar points, magnetic north and south, wandering further afield and weakening. Weakening fields can result in a proliferation of north and south magnetic poles. The Earth could have four, or eight, at the same time. Sometimes the poles nearly flip, but snap back to where they were before at the last moment. Which is to say, we know some strange things have happened in the past, but we have next to no idea what will happen in the future. We can read the history of the magnetic fields in the rocks, but we don't know how these changes affected life on the planet when they happened. We can be reasonably certain, however, that strange things are going to happen in the future.

The Earth is not the only magnet in the universe. Many of the other planets around us are also magnetic. The solar system produces magnetic storms that buffet the Earth. Solar winds buffet our magnetic shields. The force of the winds is so strong that our magnetic shield is not a spherical force field but has been blown into the shape of a tulip. When the force is strong, and if our shields are weakened, radiation escapes into the ionosphere of our planet, most often in greens but sometimes in reds and blues, giving us the glorious show of the aurora. These are most often seen at the poles, but in very strong storms they have reached into lower latitudes. The charged particles from the solar winds travel into the upper atmosphere, where ionization and excitation of the atmosphere emits lights and color.

It was the Italian astronomer Galileo Galilei who called the lights the aurora borealis in 1619, but earlier written records also described them. Greek geographer and explorer Pytheas noted them from his travels to the north in the fourth century BCE. The Stoic philosopher Seneca the Younger described them in his *Naturales quaestiones*, in 62 CE, although he lived outside their normal range in Rome and what is now Spain. Descriptions of the aurora are common in the writings of Vikings and Australian Aboriginals, perhaps more commonly seen in their higher latitudes.

The Sun is also a magnetic ball of heat and field structures. It has similar stripes of polarity, the north–south directionality of a magnet, and lines of magnetic energy that flow from south to north. When a line snaps off, it flutters about in space like a live wire before reconnecting. These snapping lines and the variable explosions of solar radiation that come with them slam into the Earth's magnetic shields. The Sun's magnetic activity has an eleven-year cycle, which affects the Earth in particular when the sun spots and coronal mass ejections peak.

Not only do planets, moons, and stars have magnetic fields and properties, they interact with each other in ways we do not really understand. In 2013, NASA discovered hidden portals in the Earth's field that created an uninterrupted path from our planet to the Sun's atmosphere, 93 million miles away. These portals appear to transfer magnet particles from Sun to Earth, creating the aurora and geomagnetic storms. The portals open and close dozens of times per day. Some are transient, and some are enormous and sustained. We don't understand much about this phenomenon either.

In the ionosphere, a wide zone of charged particles, called the Van Allen radiation belts, align to the magnetic axis of the Earth. These Van Allen belts, named for James Van Allen, the American space scientist who discovered them in 1958, are donut-shaped clouds that trap the ionized particles solar winds produce. In the South Atlantic Anomaly, the Van Allen belts come closer to the Earth's surface, and the Earth's magnetic field is weaker. This allows more radiation to escape into the atmosphere as well as to bombard satellites traveling through this part of the ionosphere. This can cause electrical glitches. These days satellites are programmed to power down in advance of reaching this area to avoid burning out their motors, and re-engage on the other side. The magnetic field at sea level in this same area is also weaker.

None of this, except the variations in measurements, was understood in the sixteenth century. Sailors may have experienced troubles but had no means by which to grasp the complexities of our planetary geophysics. Long after we began to ask the questions, we began to find answers, yet the answers haven't made it any easier to understand.

The publication of Gilbert's *Des magnete* in 1600 sent scientists further down the path of chasing the fields of this magnetic planet. His work inspired many a famous scientist to dig more deeply into these phenomena: Halley, Gauss, Alexander von Humboldt, and Charles Darwin to name a few. They would measure what was happening on the planet, and seek natural laws to explain the behaviors and models for prediction. Eventually it would also push explorers to seek and find the north and south magnetic poles. Many expeditions spent years at sea and stuck fast in ice, tracing the magnetic fields to their ends, often not returning. They sought prestige, adventure, and empire as well as naval dominance and scientific discovery. Led by men from many countries, the first of them to reach the poles were James Clark Ross (British, North Pole, 1831) and Roald Amundsen (Norwegian, South Pole, 1911).

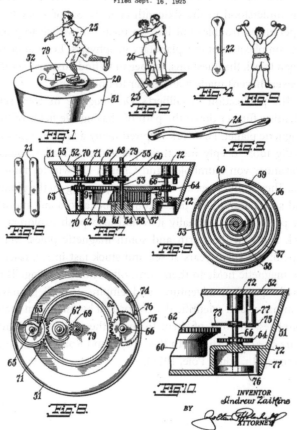

INVENTOR
Andrew Zaikine

BY

ATTORNEY

3 HOME

Humans like to explore. We have hunted and foraged, explored, crusaded, and traveled beyond the edges of our worlds. We have gone off to seek new lands, to expand our horizons, and to see what we can see. Merchants travel for commerce; explorers to find new things. People leave home for different reasons, but they all—usually—want to return.

Most early mariners followed routes that hugged the shore. Sight gave them familiar coastlines during the day, and the constellations at night. Sailing in bad weather was dangerous. The fogs of winter and the monsoons of summer kept ships in port. The navigators were part magician, part alchemist, and part astronomer. It was the navigators who knew the sea and sky, and for desert crossings, the sand and the sky. Before tools, travelers relied on skill, experience, and luck to get home. The magnetic compass provided another tool to find their way home, one deemed so important it necessitated the creation of new regulations. An injunction against navigators eating garlic at sea sprung from the belief that rubbing a magnet with garlic would take away its powers. The offense was punishable by death.

The troubles with the compass were manifold, however. The needle pointed north and south, but it was disrupted on land, and even more so at sea, and no one knew why. Early compasses were particularly fragile. The first compasses were made by magnetizing an iron needle and hanging it from a silk thread. This may work great if you are sitting still, but in motion it is hard to keep steady, and at sea with the pitch and roll of a ship it was even more complicated. Later compasses were encased in round boxes with the directional rosette drawn. While these were less fragile than a lone needle, complications remained: the metal in the ship, iron ore deposits in surrounding rocks, the numerous as yet inexplicable planetary anomalies.

From the third century BCE until the fifteenth century CE Arabs controlled the trade from Bahrain to Yemen and across to China, into the Mediterranean and across to Gibraltar. This was the maritime silk road. Records clearly show that Arab sailors used magnetic compasses in the eighth century. They were master navigators, sailing the seas in their dhows. Ahmad Ibn Majid (1421–1500) is one of the most famed for his navigational skills, even rumored to have helped Vasco da find his way to India in 1498. He left substantial writings on navigation in the form of a 1082-verse poem about astronomy, meteorology, geography, boats, and navigation.[1] His book of navigation, *The Book of Useful Information*, explicates a different model of thinking than the western sailors, the parts the world is split into, and how they measure. He notes how Europeans cannot navigate using the Arab model, but that

Arabs can use theirs. He was born in 1421, the year Zheng He's ships docked in Jeddah. Zheng He was one of the great mariners of China, reputed to have crossed the globe in his treasure ships, some of which were large enough to look like container ships, 440 feet long by 180 feet wide. (For comparison, Columbus's largest ship, the *Santa Maria*, was 62 feet by 41 feet.) He sailed in the early fifteenth century, leading seven enormous expeditions as far as Africa. Some popular books suggest he made it to Central America (most experts say no, but art and artifacts found in Mexico with styles that could be argued to be Chinese keep these rumors going).

China's early writings on the magnetic compass start not with travel but with oracles. They include the previously mentioned south-pointing soup spoon used for divination, and the compass used for Feng Shui. Soon enough, the Chinese are also using the magnetic compass for maritime trade and for desert crossings. In China, as with astronomers, the compass needle points south. (It is written that north is an inauspicious direction. Thus the emperor sits in the north, facing south, and looks across all that is his. His subjects are not so unfortunate that they are looking north, rather, they are looking up at the sky, where the emperor is above them.)

Shen Gua is one of the earliest writers on the maritime compass. In his *Dream Pool Essays* published in 1088 he collects information and catalogs it with comments. His entry on the compass follows a passage on a glowing white spaceship that visits on a regular basis. In the mid-1940s, British biochemist, historian and sinologist Joseph Needham produced an extraordinary multivolume work entitled *Science and Civilisation in China*. Needham had spent years in China exploring Chinese writings and his account includes early writings on the maritime compass, and early use of the land compass to cross the Gobi Desert.

Needham also provides greater details on the creation of the forty-pointed luopan, the compass used for Feng Shui. Feng Shui is the art, or perhaps science, of finding the optimal alignment of basically everything—furniture, walls, doorways, mirrors, houses, cities. Finding home in a metaphorical manner, the magnetic luopan allowed a home to be best aligned for an auspicious future.

There are, of course, conflicting claims as to who was the first to use the magnetic compass. Most people seem confident their own culture had it first, regardless of whether any record exists to prove them right. (Except for Francis Bacon, who was certain it was the Chinese.) And we have seen the examples of the use of a lodestone in cultures from which there is no written record, so who is to know who discovered it when, and how it was used?

Vikings were likely among the early users of a magnetic compass. Their extensive travels west across the north Atlantic and their encampments in Iceland, Greenland and Vinland support this hypothesis. As does a fragment from the Norwegian Are Frode, who in 1068, writes of Viking exploration in 868 that did not yet use the lodestone but had to follow the pole star instead. It is questionable if these navigators were trying to get home, as the Vikings dug in and set up settlements in many of their new locations, regardless of how cold, icy, or barren.

In the twelfth century the compass finally appears in European texts, first in the writings of Alexander Neckham, then of Guiot of Provins. By the 1500s there is adequate evidence to suggest that all seafaring nations of Europe and Asia were using the magnetic compass. A common language emerges across these cultures to describe the behaviors of the compass, and treatises explained its use and how to best use it in concert with other navigational information and instruments to accurately find one's way. There was variance in these methods, but not significantly so. The technology had reached around the world.

The compass helped mariners and merchants find their way to faraway lands and then return home. It also aligned us to our metaphorical homes. From long ago humans wrote of finding their true north—the meaning, calling, and passion of their existence. We've taken the language of the compass to heart, quite literally, as our heart's desire is another meaning of true north.

As new technologies evolved the magnetic compass would find new challenges. Airplanes, metal ships, fast cars, and submarines would all pose new and unexpected troubles for what began its life as a fragile device. Without an understanding of what caused the inconsistencies with the compass, it would not matter what maps, standards, or sea charts were created. In order to find their way, humans would eventually have to discover why they could not.

1,064,914.

Patented June 17, 1913.

2 SHEETS—SHEET 1.

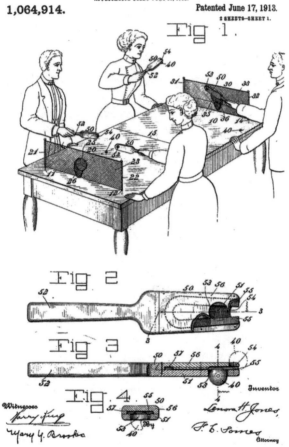

Fig 1.

Fig 2.

Fig 3.

Fig 4.

Witnesses

Inventor

Lenora H. Jones,

Attorney

4 ALIGNMENT

The complexity of the problems in the search for and exploration of biological effects of magnetic fields is almost overwhelming.

NASA TECHNICAL NOTE, TN D-5902, 1970

Humans are pretty good at getting lost, especially in the age of urbanization, smartphones, and GPS. Some still have a sense of directionality, learned by rote, from traveling the same paths day after day. But the more humans regularly rely on devices rather than knowledge and experience, the less we seem able to find our way without them.

We've left behind the skills of the ancient navigators, the abilities to align to the stars or the Sun, to know the constellations, and to identify the changes in the sky with the passing of the seasons. If you close your eyes and spin in circles, would you know which way is north when you stop? Can you use the Sun or the stars to align yourself? Do you need to follow the same route you took to a new place, or can you envision the map and take a shortcut?

In the era of maps and compasses, one had to know where one was, to orient to where one needed to be. We no longer rely on knowledge, or the magnetic compass to get from here to there, we rely on the magnets that power our smartphones and our GPS. We no longer need to know where we are to get to where we are going. The GPS takes even that knowledge away from us. We can be more lost than we ever were.

We've always been a species that builds tools to supplant where we lack for certain abilities or innate behaviors. In many nonhuman species directional knowledge is both innate and learned, in different combinations. But what of these other species? How do they find their way? More than a century ago we knew a carrier pigeon could find its way home. In ancient times both the Greeks and the Tartars used pigeons to send messages and receive replies. As recently as World War II pigeons were outfitted with cameras to take pictures of battlefields, bringing back their film to command central. Arabic writings confirm that by the twelfth century birds were used to travel long distances for sending and receiving messages.

Understanding why pigeons can do this is a recent undertaking. Early experiments involved disrupting their abilities. If magnets were attached to their feet, they could not get home. If the magnetic field was disrupted, they could not get home. Something about the magnetic fields was giving these birds information, but what that information was and how it was experienced and processed was still unknown.

Over the past fifty years more and more species have been found to have some type of biomagnetism—some type of magnetic substance in their bodies that can be used to see and/or align to the Earth's magnetic fields. In the simplest form, an animal will understand north and south alignment. You can see this in action with a field of cows. Unless disrupted by overhead power lines, cows at rest will align on a north–south line. Deer and other ruminants also do so. They do not seem to travel by these lines, but when they stop, they line up.[1]

Yet as we know, terrestrial magnetism isn't a simple thing. Animals can align to the north–south polar field, but they can also interact with intensity, and dip, and it's likely that most use a combination of these measures to know where they are, where to go, and how to get there.

In the case of pigeons, it turns out they have crystals in their beaks that align to the magnetic fields. Imagine a magnetic field as a carpet draped over a lumpy ground, with wavery weft and warp. Each carpet, in each place, is slightly different, and it marginally changes over time. An animal can align to warp or weft, to shape, or to intensity of the field, how strongly it pulls. In scientific terms, the magnetic field lines are north–south lines (with wobbles). Intensity measures the strength of the magnetic field. Dip measures the angle of the field—does it point into the Earth or away from the Earth. All of these measures change over time, as well.

To create a map of a magnetic field one could track one of those, or all, and they could be combined with other types of navigation and mapmaking, from solar or stellar alignment, landmarks, spatial relationships, wind, scent, or temperature. We know that different species use and combine these ways of knowing. Keep in mind, this is only what we know, what we can imagine. It wasn't until recently we thought to look at temples to see if they were aligned to magnetic fields, rather than stellar or solar phenomena. We may not "see" something crucial to this picture. Studying cognition, field alignment, and mapmaking in other species is difficult.

Most research is done by disrupting animals who interact with the magnetic fields, to see what can be learned by doing so. Just as scientists attached magnets to pigeons, studies have run bar magnets near magnetic bacteria, hijacked birds in dark cages to faraway places to see if they could get home, crossbred species who seem to home in to different cardinal directions, attached satellite trackers to follow pathways from space. In controlled cases the fields themselves are tweaked, varying direction, intensity, or dip to see what happens in the brains of animals. In one case, the researchers bred birds in a low magnetism environment, so they could not learn the fields as youngsters, to see if the knowledge was learned or innate. They then watched if they got lost upon their release into the wild. They did.

Biomagnetic substances have been found in crystals, proteins, and magnetosomes, across species, and in many areas of the body. They have been located in eyes, and blood, and embedded in beaks and noses and teeth. They have been found in the pineal gland. But how do they work? What these materials sense must have a pathway to the brain to create usable information. Some information seems to have pathways to the ocular nerve, whereas some appears to go nowhere.

In a recent study, a shift in a magnet field showed thirty-seven different neuronal areas firing in a bird brain, but the researchers had no idea how the birds knew this. They hypothesized that the inner ear contained some type of sense organ that transmitted the information.

And in (yet another) further complication, some species have more than one type of biomagnetic material, and use the world and other signals to know where they are and where they are going. Salmon, spiny lobsters, assorted bacteria, many species of birds—but not the albatross—ruminants, trout, zebra fish, and turtles are just some of the life-forms in which we have discovered alignment to magnetic fields. Chitons have magnetite teeth. Magnetic bacteria live in the ocean at the line between the aerobic and the anaerobic, oxygen and no oxygen. They've been hovering at that line for hundreds of thousands of years, using their internal alignment to stay on just the right side of the oxygen line. There are some early writings on plant alignment as well, and insects (though most have been recently debunked).

As far as we know, humans cannot do this, but two interesting things may leave this an open question. First, certain languages don't have words for left or right. They use only cardinal locations: the cake is to the west of me, I put the cookies on the south end of the table. Many of these languages are from the Pama-Nyungan family in Australia. The British linguist Stephen Levinson studied the speakers of the language Guugu Yimithirr and if you read of this cardinal directionality it is usually his work that is cited. In his fieldwork seeking to understand the relationship between the language and the speaker's spatial awareness, he found that subjects in rooms with no windows, in the dark, or traveling in a moving vehicle, knew which direction they were facing. It is not known how, or why. The second is the presence of a protein in the eyes of humans, which is also found in the eyes of birds who can sense magnetic fields.

Crpytochrome 4, or cry4, is a protein found in the eyes of many birds that is only activated in a particular spectrum of blue light. The leading hypothesis is that birds can only see these fields when they need to migrate. Imagine if one day, say near a holiday, you see a visible grid overlaid on your world, guiding you home. It would be something like that. Cry4 is also found in human eyes, but we have no mechanism for any information it may generate to travel to our brains. When scientists took cry4 from human eyes, placed it in magnetic bacteria, and bathed them in blue light, the bacteria did begin to travel north. So it works, it just doesn't work for us. As far as we know.

Behaviors that align to the magnetic fields include annual migrations, daily travels, and that once-in-a-lifetime return to the spawning grounds to breed. Combine all of these different possibilities together and you have a soup of complexity for animal interaction with magnetic fields. Imagine you are a robin that wants to head south for the winter. How do you know where to go? Two different answers have been found. One is an innate alignment passed from parent to offspring. Your parents went south for the winter, you go south, your parents went west for the winter, you go west. This example is real and was found in two different species of European robin. When placed in a darkened lab in Germany with no visual clues, the west-facing robins aligned to the west and the south-facing robins aligned to the south when it came time for their annual migration. When scientists crossbred the birds, these new offspring reportedly faced southwest, and so the scientists did not release them, as they would have flown over the Atlantic and died. The published paper is reasonable, but the thought exercise is crazy. To believe this is true one must look at directionality as an additive property. If I combine west (270°) and south (180°) the outcome will be the average of the two, southwest (225°). This is as bizarre, perhaps, as believing that the continents slide around the planet on plates and have previously been in different shapes. It is so strange, directionality as a mathematical property innate to the navigation skills of a species, that I fear I shall return for the journal article and it will simply have disappeared from the internet, that years of thinking about magnets and planetary alignment produced this craziness.

Loggerhead turtles are by far the most complex in their behaviors and one of the most difficult to study. These turtles can weigh up to one thousand pounds and travel thousands of miles when it comes time to spawn. It has long been thought they used sophisticated navigational skills to do so, but it was hard to track a thousand-pound turtle over thousands of miles. Scientists have since attached chips to the turtles' shells so they can track their migrations via satellite, but this doesn't tell us how they are navigating. We can look for correlations to the field, seeking patterns that may give us information, but this is different from knowing. Turtles understand the magnetic field enough to find their way back to the beaches where they were born. This means they understand the shape of the field that existed before they were born, and probably even the history of the field, so that as it changes, they still know where they are going. When they are born, the field—declination, dip, and intensity—becomes part of the magnetic map in their brains. The young hatchlings can travel with fair precision to a place thousands of miles away that they have never seen nor been. And let's not forget, those dogs circling about? Research on these behaviors show that dogs prefer to poop to the north. Daily fluctuations in the magnetic field make the fields more difficult to sense at certain times of day, so if you wonder why sometimes it takes your pup a while to choose his spot, blame the magnetic field.

In 2008, NASA's Wind spacecraft measured the magnetic field created by the solar winds as they rush across space. They took these data files and transformed them into audio files, assigning sounds to fluctuations to bring them into the range of human hearing, much like a Geiger counter is the sonification of radiation levels. People listened to these files and could easily pick out subtle differences in the variations of the patterns. Which is to say, we can hear the magnetic fields. Perhaps it is not just that the inner ear in some birds have crystals to sense the fields, but some species can actually hear them too.

One final story on animal alignment to terrestrial magnetism is perhaps the oddest yet. Quantum magnetics is a baffling space and I am not going to go too deep into it here. Best to find a physicist and have her give it a whirl. Bioethologists discovered that it wasn't crystal or protein in the eyes of the European robin that allowed them to see the magnetic field structure, but rather quantum entanglement, such that the two strands of being found themselves across space-time and re-paired back where they belong. This is what Einstein called "spooky action at a distance." A German scientist, Klaus Schulten (1947–2016), found that these entangled particles are "extraordinarily sensitive to both the strength and orientation of magnetic fields." He proposed this as the explanation for why certain birds can find their way: they have a quantum-entangled compass in their eyes, and are connected to the place they need to get to. His theory is beginning to find traction with ornithologists Wolfgang and Roswitha Wiltschko, who have found compelling experimental evidence to support Schulten's hypothesis.

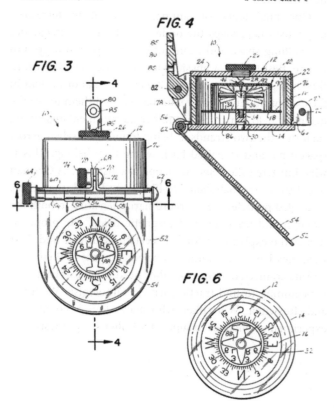

FIG. 4

FIG. 3

FIG. 6

5 NORTH

It complicates our understanding of a magnet to have north and south poles as well as a planet with north and south poles—two sets of both, one magnetic and one geographic. Energy flows out of the north pole of a magnet and into the south, opposite poles attract, and like poles repel. These are the fundamental dynamics of a bar magnet. Even though we know the Earth does not have a bar magnet in its center, it is likely how most of us think of the planet. North, up, magnetic north. South, down, magnetic south. The poles of the magnet, however, are not geographic, but descriptive. They describe the flow of energy rather than cardinal directions. The northern geographic magnetic pole is actually a south pole; the energy flows into the north.

Add to the mix the concept of a magnetic axis as well, currently eleven degrees off the geographic north pole. The north magnetic pole and the south magnetic pole are not directly opposite from each other, as much as we might imagine an axis through the Earth being a straight line. We also have a magnetic equator, which is not the same as *the* equator, but flows a bit north, and south, in an inconsistent imaginary line around the Earth. We've laid out a complicated language for ourselves, in the duplication of terms meaning not quite the same things.

The northern geographic pole is fixed. It is a point on the spheroid that is our planet. The magnetic north pole is more of a field, less a point, and it is not fixed. In the course of a day, the north pole's diurnal variation can deviate as much as eighty kilometers from the mean. It took a while for scientists and explorers to realize this was the case, which explains why it was so hard to find a second time, and so easy to deny it was found before.

In the nineteenth century, scientists and explorers were *still* on the hunt for the natural laws of magnetism, the ability to predict the behaviors of terrestrial magnetism. The work of their predecessors had provided key information, such as the knowledge of the westward drift, local magnetic anomalies, and the makeup of the interior of the Earth. They had created seafaring maps and land survey maps of much greater detail and fidelity. But several things still eluded them. No one had located magnetic north or south, the auroras were poorly understood, and there was no set of natural laws that governed magnetism. The great seafaring nations also felt that both enhanced tools and the national honor of locating the poles would support a world that was continuing to turn toward empire, conquest, colonization, and trade.

In England, the ideologies of empire combined with cartography and commerce, sending ships to sea. Science was bullish and several expeditions were sent forth to seek an understanding of terrestrial magnetism, either to solve the "longitude problem" or driven by an enormous curiosity about this mysterious force.

Oxford began to teach geography classes to English students who understood the map, the globe, and desired to head out into the wilds. These students were trained in mathematical cartography, a way of quantifying the known world, and from them would come a generation of "observers," the record-keepers who went to sea with the captains and natural historians to record the world as they found it. And, perhaps, to stick a flag in some unknown land and claim it for queen and country. For the England of the time, this created an idea of British exceptionalism, embodied in their maps and their expeditions. These students were a new class of quantifiers, and with their knowledge of observations and mathematics, they were also learning of the primacy of England. They would go out in the world, and then come home to rule. They understood the importance of the compass and survey tools, and the ways in which knowledge would give them a leg up.

In the race for the poles, sights were first set on the north. Perhaps because it was closer to the nations in question, or perhaps because it was on the way to finding the Northwest Passage. The Northwest Passage was a route of great importance, a way to reach the riches of Asia without having to sail south around the cape. North was also a mythical space, originally a dark, cold northern land full of giants, dragons, and danger. The desire for acclaim sent sailors and adventurers out on the ships, often funded and supported by the Admiralty, when national interests as well as scientific ones were at hand.

The first ships to search for the Northwest Passage usually included an astronomer to take measurements, both of the sky and the magnetic fields. It would take several tries before the route was found, and many died, including Captain John Franklin's disastrous expedition when all 138 men and his ships were lost. Before Franklin, James Clark Ross successfully located the north magnetic pole, or at least got close enough to count at the time. He is generally credited with being first, even though he, and Amundsen who was to return there just over fifty years later, both hedge. It is hard to be definitive about something inconsistent.

In 1829 Ross embarked upon what would be a four-year voyage. Funding expeditions was difficult, as ships, crew, and instruments, as well as provisions were expensive. Felix Booth, purveyor of Booth's Gin, gave twenty thousand pounds to Ross's expedition, thus we have Boothia Bay. He was a seasoned sailor and had been on Arctic excursions before. These prior excursions, both by his father and by others, had provided key observations that allowed Ross to narrow the area in which he would look for the pole. Like most polar expeditions, the trip was not an easy one. Ross successfully located the pole near Boothia Bay in what is now Nunavut at roughly 70°N and 96°W, though later writers dispute this. The measurements they took, in June of 1831, showed that they were one degree short of the pole, but given the diurnal movement of the pole, they assumed they had found the spot.

In December of 1833 Ross read his paper "On the Position of the North Magnetic Pole" at the Royal Society of London. His paper tells the tale of a trip fraught with difficulties but the writing itself is very matter-of-fact, taking the errors and issues in stride. After acknowledging the importance and difficulty of understanding magnetism, and to those who came before and failed, Ross then launched into a description of the tools they brought with them. In the first of many troubles, he writes, "It is, however, to be regretted, that prior to our departure from England we had no opportunity of making any observations with that instrument; and a defect which was not detected until spring of the year 1831, has rendered it necessary to reject all observations on the intensity of the magnetic force made previous to that period" (48).

In describing their rapid approach toward the magnetic pole, he notes "we were unconscious at that time of the existence of an ocean in that direction, and the calculated distance far exceeded anything we could hope to travel whose rugged shores seemed to forbid the attempt, and to annihilate every hope of its accomplishment" (48–49). And a further disaster: "An azimuth compass was the only magnetic instrument that could be taken, and this was, soon after leaving the ship, destroyed by a fall over a precipice at Cape Isabella." They were then forced to overwinter in that spot, and continue on in May of 1831 in the direction they had marked as their heading, before the demise of the compass.

To mark their direction, they used a magnetized needle suspended from silk. They did eventually find the pole and mark it as magnetic north using dip measurements, though even Ross suggests that although they were in the vicinity, it would be hard to be explicit of the exact point. The paper closes with an admonishment to carry on additional operations given that they are now within easy access to the spot. He says, "It is certainly every way worthy of our country. The science of magnetism, indeed, is eminently British." It would be more than fifty years until a British-funded expedition returned to this point, though soon after Ross heads to the south pole, charged to find the magnetic pole in the southern hemisphere. The British Antarctic Expedition traveled for four years, 1839 to 1844. The mission was purely scientific, Ross's directions were "to improve the science of magnetism" by "proceed[ing] direct to the southward, in order to determine the position of the magnetic pole, and even to attain it if possible."[1] This voyage was a success. It disproved Halley's hypothesis that there were two southern magnetic poles, in addition to finding the southern magnetic pole itself.

Many of the greatest scientists of the time went to sea as magnetic observers, set up observatories, and rushed to collect the data that would provide them with the natural laws of magnetism. Gauss and Humboldt were fast at work on terrestrial magnetism in the 1830s and 1840s. Humboldt was setting up the "*maisons magnetiques*" from Paris and Gauss was doing the same from Gottingen, Germany. Edward

Sabine, who had been an astronomer for one of Ross's trips to seek the Northwest Passage, was a strong advocate in England for the creation of a focused effort to understand terrestrial magnetism. He, along with William Parry and others, were the driving force behind the Magnetic Crusade, a title perhaps originally given in jest, but eventually taking hold for almost half a century of focus.

Following the Magnetic Conference of 1845, the Admiralty caved to public and institutional pressure to support the continued terrestrial magnetic endeavors. The scientific discoveries came hard and fast in the following decades, and the scientists were heaped with national glory.

Amundsen began arguing the case for further exploration to the north pole at the turn of the twentieth century, seeking backers and funding. He wrote two articles for the Royal Geographical Society. In "A Proposed Expedition to the North Magnetic Pole," published in April of 1902, he explains the basics of the science and what they are trying to do, and recaps prior voyages. He does a particularly clear job of this. On Ross's expedition he writes:

James Ross thus arrived on June 1, 1831, at a spot where the dipping-needle showed an angle of 89° 59' with the plane of the horizon—in other words, was only deflected one minute from an absolutely vertical position. Practically this one minute is of little consequence, and Ross himself considered that he had now really reached the magnetic pole, whose geographical position he accurately determined to be 70° 5′ N. lat., 96° 47′ W. long.; and, satisfied with this result, he ceased all further investigations, and has thus contributed nothing towards the solution of the question that has since presented itself, namely, whether the magnetic pole is actually only a point, or whether possibly the peculiarity of the needle assuming a vertical position extends over a large area. Theoretical study of recent times points decidedly to the latter supposition. Another question that also demands a practical solution, and which I have already briefly touched upon, is whether the magnetic pole is stationary, or changes its position. It is the solution of these two questions that I have set myself the task of attempting.

He continues on to describe his ship, equipment, and methods. His second article, "Expedition to the North Magnetic Pole," was published in December of the same year. He had intended to self-fund his expedition and was in the process of gathering these funds himself, when his first article resulted in external funding and thus he could sail earlier than expected. He published a declaration of his planned path, a timeline, and the expectations of completion. It was to be a multiyear trip with the expectation that they must overwinter, though he chose a small ship that he hoped could escape being stuck in the ice too early.

In 1903, Amundsen and his tiny ship with seven crew sailed, spending eighteen months seeking magnetic north and then the Northwest Passage. They overwintered near where Ross had located the magnetic north pole, taking measurements for the season and awaiting a turn in the weather that would allow them to reach the pole themselves. During this time period they made two attempts to reach magnetic north, but both were aborted due to the weather. When the ship was freed from the ice in 1905 they headed west, making their way to Nome, Alaska, before returning. They returned to Oslo in 1906, where Amundsen planned to head again to seek magnetic north; however he scrapped this plan when Robert Peary announced in that he had located it, and turned his sights to the south pole.[2] The American claimed to have reached magnetic north in 1909, though it was widely debated at the time. Eventually he was given credit, but then in the 1980s it was fairly well disproved, though he did make it close, within seventy miles.

Since that time the magnetic north pole has traveled across Arctic Canada, heading toward Russia at the pace of about fifty kilometers per year. (One can't but wonder what Putin will do with it when it "becomes Russian.") Historical research shows the path of the magnetic north back two hundred years, wobbling about in Northern Canada.

Expeditions were undertaken and additional magnetic observatories were set up in the high northern latitudes to continue these observations. Two-person teams spend months if not years at a time in what looks like small shacks in the tundra, making observations and sending them back for analysis. They have existed for hundreds of years, and still do. The observations measure declination and horizontal force, dip, and transit. For hundreds of years those were the basic measures, though today we have more advanced technology to take additional measures, including measurements taken off-planet by satellites.

North is an interesting concept, a position on the map, but a metaphorical connection to the compass, directions, and ways of seeing the world. Before the sixteenth century, maps varied in which direction would be on top. Christian maps had east at the top, the direction of Jerusalem. East was also the direction of the rising Sun, and as such had importance. In many languages, the words for the cardinal directions related to the rising and the setting of the Sun. Whether we oriented in space, or with a map, the first point, the place we first looked to, in the day, varied by place, language, and culture. We have extended the metaphor of north to mean industrialized, productive, wealth, forward-thinking.

Why would one want to locate the magnetic north or south pole? We have incredible tales of daring to find them, but why remains a valid question. What did these nations think they would do with these spots on a globe when they were located? And why would so many people die to find these magnetic nadirs? We know where they are, and magnetic observatories still exist in the highest latitudes, manned by one or two people for a few months at a time. We can take readings by hand and by machine, and even by satellite. It is still hard to say what we *do* with them, though. The knowledge of the magnetic points allows maps to be updated to have the correct declination, allowing someone using a map and a traditional compass to orienteer, to set their sights and travel, knowing that the true north of the map is off by eleven degree east, or eight degrees west, based on one's position in the world.

We use these points to align technology and equipment as well, devices that need magnets to work must be calibrated and aligned to the field. In the meantime, we continue to track, to follow, and to gather data. Perhaps, like the sound of a gravity wave, we will one day discover something completely unexpected, simply because we were listening.

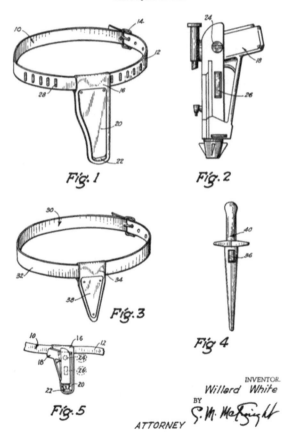

Fig. 1

Fig. 2

Fig. 3

Fig 4

Fig. 5

INVENTOR.

Willard White

BY

G. M. McKnight

ATTORNEY

6 HEALTH

Early medical treatises discussed health in terms of constitutional flows within a body, the humors of Greece, the meridians of China, the *doshas* of India. These substances could be out of balance, causing illness. The four bodily humors—black bile, yellow bile, blood, and phlegm—could be in excess or deficient. The *doshas—vata, pitta*, and *kappa*—could be out of balance, and the meridians and pulses of Chinese medicine could be weak. A patient's temperament was based upon the makeup of the elements, and the goal of medicine was to keep them in balance lest illness arise.

In early medical treatises physicians learned that the magnet could be used to treat a variety of ills. In Greece, the stone was classified as cold and dry, and so it was used to generate those properties. It could thus cool the overly hot and dry the overly moist. It was pressed into bleeding wounds to stem the flow of blood and used to stop semen from escaping the uterus of a woman. It was also believed to reduce the moistness of women, something thought to cause all sorts of troubles, from infertility to insanity.

While the physicians were diagnosing and treating, the surgeons found a different use for the stone. Surgical guides first appeared in 600 BCE that mentioned the use of *ayas kantra* ("iron love") to remove arrowheads. The Ayurvedic surgery guide compiled by Sucruta covered the use of magnets for more than just removing metal, including treatments for megacolon and other advanced diseases. Nearly two thousand years later, in 1290, Gilbertus Anglicus writes about surgeons using the magnet if "iron is concealed in the flesh."

Starting in ancient times, people strapped magnets to the body in the belief it would stop bleeding or dampen pain. This belief originated in Greece but writings from the Japanese and the Europeans also note this use. Gaps in writing and "new" discoveries suggest this knowledge was often lost, and rediscovered. In the eighteenth century, the astronomer and Jesuit monk Maximilian Hell strapped magnets to his joints in an attempt to alleviate arthritis pain. It was also standard treatment in Chinese medicine at the time. A quick search of the internet today will produce numerous sites selling magnet cures for the same pain. Recent scientific studies have shown that applying magnetic fields to bone fractures will speed healing.

Franz Anton Mesmer introduced the vocabulary of the magnetic force, of animal magnetism, to the wider world in the mid eighteenth century. (More on him in the next chapter.) Mesmer also introduced the mesmeric trance, a form of manipulation of the magnetic fields within a human being more closely aligned now to hypnosis than to magnetism. In the eighteenth and nineteenth centuries surgeons used this magnetically induced trance to perform "pain-free" surgery.

In 1851 James Esdaile, a Scottish surgeon with the East India Company, wrote a very descriptive book about his mesmeric practice at a country charity hospital in Bengal. In it he describes amputations performed under mesmeric trance as a method of anesthesia. His book, sent to his father in England, seems a bit more of a mix of adventure and gore rather than a medical treatise and, I hope, overstates the work that he did. In addition to his numerous amputations, including the removal of fourteen scrotal tumors "weighing from 8lb to 80lb," he can also cure the "feeling of insects crawling over one's body" in a single trance.

A psychological focus of the origins of disease was put forth by Paracelsus in the sixteenth century. His metaphysical perspective on the theory of disease suggested that all corporeal changes originated in the imagination, the animating spirit of nature. He believed the heavens were the source of our sickness, and within our minds we had the ability to transform our bodies, that the "seeds of disease" are planted in the imagination and that we make the disease real.

DARPA has been investing significant money into the ElectRX program, seeking to find ways in which the body can use magnetic fields to stimulate the brain into treating illnesses. They believe self-induced treatment, under the heading of magnetogenetics, will allow us to shift our internal structures, for the better.

Researchers at MIT are exploring ways to create magnetic nanoparticles that will bind to specific neurons to activate those neurons. How these will heal us or allow us to heal ourselves is not yet clear, but it is reminiscent of the magnetic water Mesmer believed flowed through all people, which allowed the body to be manipulated to recognize what was wrong and heal itself.

Entwined with old writings on the use of magnets for healing and in surgery are those on the use of magnets for magic. In Greek mythology, the Daktyloi were gods of a class of divinities called *daimones*. They were ecstatic male dancers, magicians, and metallurgists. Daktyloi came in two varieties: those who used their power to increase fertility and those who used it to squelch it. The Daktyloi were worshipped in metal, in amulets, in rings, a god of pharmacy and fecundity. Women who wished to become pregnant made amulets in Heracles' honor and recited incantations. For less permanent assistance, people wrapped magnets and incantations in cloth around the parts of the body they wanted the Daktyloi to heal, magnet and incantation combined in one. Perhaps the Dakytloi were the precursor to the Jesuits and the Chinese using a similar treatment, and today, the internet is full of offers of magnets that can be worn to treat pain.

The *Orphic Lithica*, a fourth-century treatise on mineralogy and the use of stones, includes a magical use of the stone to generate desire, perhaps based upon the attracting behaviors of the stone itself.

In the 1980s, transcranial magnetic stimulation (TMS) emerged as a method of diagnostics and therapy. It has been used to diminish cocaine cravings in drug addicts, treat depression, and change one's moral stances. The affect the magnets change depend on which part of the brain is stimulated, and for how long, both at a go, and over time.

William Crookes, the future president of the Royal Society, published a paper in 1892 suggesting it might be possible for thoughts to transmit from mind to mind through the electromagnetic ether. Current research believes that zapping the brain with magnetic pulses while measuring its electrical activity may be used to detect consciousness. Doctors are using this on severely brain-injured patients to inform decision-making about care.

These only scratch the surface of the ways in which magnets are being used or studied in the field of medicine. Other topics include geomagnetic activity and human melatonin metabolite excretion; a role for the geomagnetic field in cell regulation; and magnetic field effect on neurite outgrowth.

In history, the magnetic fields of people have been aligned to phrenology, to the sky, to celestial events, and we have even gone so far as to drink iron filings to allow these fluids to move about the body. Body hackers in the modern era have embedded magnets in their fingers, to acquire an additional sense. (I'm told it feels like wiggling beneath the skin, to sense a magnetic field.) To what end, it is hard to say.

Field resonance was once considered to be woo, but now science is beginning to provide data to show that humans do have magnetic fields and we do resonate with those around us. Our brains and our hearts generate magnetic fields, fields that can align. Move close to a loved one, and your hearts will combine fields and share their oscillations. I recall a speaker many years ago saying, "The magnetic resonance of the Earth is the same as the alpha waves in the brain," and he continued, "We can feel this level or resonance, connection, and love. To sync up with another, you must be within five feet of another person." I don't know if this was true, but science seems to be catching up to him.

With the advent of low-magnetic field rooms, where the ambient magnetism of the planet is removed, we have discovered that both the heart and the brain resonate with magnetic fields, and that in close enough proximity to others, these fields will sync up. Studies of pregnant women in these low-magnetic field environments can detect the different but in sync magnetic resonances of the hearts of mama and babe.

The magic of the Middle Ages is recorded in so many places, and even a small sampling is a pleasure to read. The magnet was thought to make the invisible visible and if it was placed under a pillow, it would expose an adulterous woman. She would be expelled forcefully from her bed had she been untrue. A few of the things curable by magnets, gathered from Thorndike's *History of Magic and Experimental Science* include: Augustine believed the blood of a goat could break the hold of a magnet; Berthelot believed it was a key ingredient for an alchemist's creation of gold; Peregrinus believed the magnet could be used to drive away crows and to tell if a person is a leper; Peter of Abano believed a magnet taken internally produced melancholy and insanity. Thorndike's eight-volume history is rife with millennia of beliefs.

Humans are not the only species for whom magnets are used for medical care. Ranchers put magnets in stomach number one of free-range cows, which apparently is the strongest of the lot, to keep any metal the cow may eat stuck in the first stomach so it will not pass further into the system and harm the cow. The ranchers pass these magnets into their stomachs using tubes.

We know that magnetic fields affect cows and other ruminants, overhead power lines disrupting their normally aligned lives. There is substantive scientific literature demonstrating that physiological regulatory systems in animals and humans are affected by and even synchronized to the magnetic fields of the Earth. Disruptions in these fields have been observed to create adverse effects on health and behavior. Researchers (usually in the pay of the creators of these fields) say the fields do not harm humans, while at the same time research shows these same fields cause genetic and epigenetic harm in children. We know so little about how magnetism and magnetic fields played a part in the evolutionary process of life on Earth, save the navigational techniques previously mentioned, that it is hard to know what effects magnets and magnetism have on our health and well-being.

Medical imaging allows us to see inside the body. In the 1970s magnetic resonance imaging (MRI) introduced a far better way to see within, supplanting X-rays. It could discriminate between soft tissue and allowed for earlier diagnoses. fMRI was born, the functional MRI that allows us to see what happens in our brains when we do something, to map action to brain activity, to see what we think, or what we believe. It gives us a better view of what is happening in our brains when we apply magnets or magnetic fields to our brains or bodies.

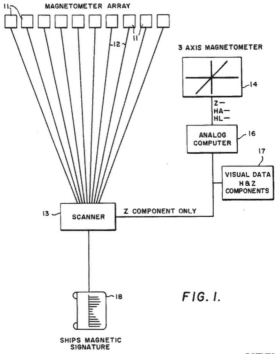

FIG. 1.

INVENTOR

WAYNE E. BURT

BY   *Howard W. Hermann*

AGENT.

7 TRANSCENDENCE

Franz Anton Mesmer came to Vienna in 1759 to study medicine. He brought with him a new healing technique relying upon "animal magnetism" and the magnetic fluid he believed ran in all humans. He described this fluid as all-knowing, a fluid that one brought to the fore with an induced trance, which would allow the body to identify its illness and heal itself. His protocol went through several rounds. In the early days, perhaps taken from his study with Maximilian Hell, he waved magnets over the bodies of his patients. In Vienna it is said that patients first drank water with iron filings in it, so that the magnets he ran across their bodies would call to the magnetic elements inside. Later, he forgoes both magnetic water and magnets, claiming he is strong enough to control the magnetic fluid with his hands alone.

Mesmer and his animal magnetism took Vienna by storm. He married an older, wealthy widow who gave him entrée into society, and began to hold treatment salons. He treated Maria Theresia von Paradis, a blind pianist who was a favorite of the queen, temporarily curing her (though disastrously resulting in the loss of her skills as a musical prodigy, and putting Mesmer on the bad side of the queen. Eventually things reverted: she re-lost her sight and regained her musical skills).

Accounts of Mesmer's treatment describe him calling out the magnetic fluid to bring a patient to crisis. The crisis involved shaking, sobbing, and seizures. From Vienna, he moved on to Paris as a wunderkind of modern healing, and set up a new salon, with much pomp and flamboyance. These sessions were accompanied by the show of a well-practiced stage performer: a cape, a bath, harp music, metal bars, held at an expensive address. He had the love of the aristocracy, and the disdain of the scientific establishment. A faint odor of scandal circled around these sessions, but for Mesmer acolytes, there was no turning back.

In the late eighteenth century people were hungry for something, for an escape from their lives, for meaning, for a way to belong in the world. Mesmer offered this. He described his magnetic fluid as one that aligns to the stars, suggesting that the fluid is a universal substance that connected one to oneself and others. The etchings of his salons are intimate, people letting go of conventions and constraints as they descend into trances and fits. Whatever the cause, perhaps merely suggestion, the idea of being cosmically connected to the universe appeals and his magnetism takes.

Mesmer's dream was to have his technique recognized by the Royal Academy of Medicine, to have his science be recognized as such, but he was from the wrong class for this, and his only recognition came from his aristocratic clientele.

The lack of validation distressed him to no end and in spite of his growing power in society, he decided to quit Paris. Upon hearing the news, Marie Antoinette, an avowed Mesmerist, offered him a clinic and a stipend to remain.

He agreed to stay, but his growing power attracted attention. The king assembled a panel to prove he was a fraud, which they do, and Mesmer is sent off into exile. But the magnetic fluid, animal magnetism, and mesmerism lived on, not just in our metaphorical language. Factions of Mesmer's students continue to treat patients with his hands-on technique, and practitioners brought it to England and the United States. Mesmer also gave birth to a movement, of a way to be in the world; he wasn't healing physical ills so much as existential ones. Patients gave themselves over to his power, he ran his hands over them, they entered a crisis, writhing and screaming and begging, and then, when they came back to themselves, they were physically and spiritually healed. The writings of the time don't speak of angst or misery or the difficulties of life. They speak of physical ills.

Mesmerism and animal magnetism reached America as a cross between a sideshow and a church revival. Stage performers showed off their skills to crowds who oohed and aahed, more an escape from daily life in the form of entertainment than healing or transcendence. The medical establishment picks it up and transforms it for surgery, not just Dr. Esdaile but others as well, which in turn shifts from mesmerism to hypnotism. In England Mesmer's numerous practitioners adopt magnetism and eventually it finds its way to the Theosophists. Madame Blavatsky, cofounder of the Theosophical Society, wrote about it, and it made its way into the writings of Christian Science founder Mary Baker Eddy. Theologian Emanuel Swedenborg also engaged in similar concepts, with each group taking the magnetic cure as its starting point, and then shifting it as they saw fit.

According to the historian Robert Darnton, Mesmer and his theories had much farther-reaching effects than introducing a new science of health and healing to French society. Mesmer's inability to be accepted by the scientists of the Royal Academy introduced a revolutionary strain to his work as he was accepted by the queen and aristocracy, and suggested that there could be a path of inclusion by those not born of the proper class. Jean-Paul Marat was in a similar situation, where his experiments on physics were not given the weight he deserved. Darnton believes that the language of mesmerism, and the beliefs that went with it, revolutionized his followers and became part of the ethos of the French Revolution.

One of the most famous residents of Bedlam, the insane asylum in London, James Tilly Matthews believed he suffered from mind control caused by a machine called an "air loom," which warped magnetic fields and could be used to control anyone. He left drawings of the air loom, and other details, including his belief that Jacobin terrorists had implanted a magnet in his brain to make this easier. The gang of terrorists also possessed magnetized batons that could be used to cloud the perception of those around them. Perhaps a precursor to the twenty-first-century studies showing a magnetic field applied to the brain could changes one's moral beliefs?

There is research that suggests magnetic stimulation of certain parts of the brain can speed one's path to enlightenment. fMRI scans show a pattern that is similar to those of monks and long-term meditators. Papers suggest that using magnetic resonance to move our brain into those shapes should make us feel the same. What would it be like if we could use these fields that surround us to diagnose and heal ourselves, change our moral views, and invoke a happy and fulfilling life? It sounds like there is a magnetic utopia ahead, if true.

1,171,972.

Patented Feb. 15, 1916.

Fig. 1.

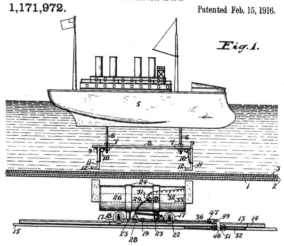

Fig. 3.

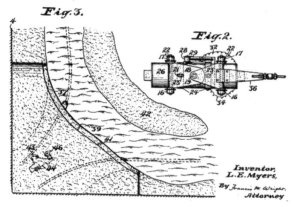

Fig. 2.

Inventor,
L. E. Myers,
By *Francis M. Wright*
Attorney

8 TRICKS

On September 1, 1859, British astronomer Richard Carrington noticed a coronal mass ejection on the Sun, a burst of solar wind and magnetic energy we now associate with Sun flares and solar plasma. This massive explosion resulted in auroras seen as far south as San Salvador and Honolulu. It disrupted the telegraph system across the world, giving off electric sparks. In 1967, another enormous geomagnetic storm disrupted global communications technologies. It jammed America's surveillance technologies, leading the U.S. government to believe the Soviet Union was engaged in acts of war. (Another Carrington event of this size could disrupt the global communications infrastructure for years.) Geophysical phenomena plays its tricks on us—polar reversals, roving polar locations, and the multiplication of "norths" and "souths" as the fields weaken—but humans have a few tricks up their sleeves as well.

Ancient magnetic fantasies ranged from levitating gods to magnetic mountains to ships that are torn apart when the nails are ripped from their hulls as they pass a magnetic island. The Romans and the Chinese have stories of magnetic battlements that attract interlopers like flies or tear weapons from hands. Ancient Ethiopia has tales of how magnets could be used to tear ore from the Earth, with miners watching along, no human intervention necessary.

There are modern tales of magnetic superheroes, ways to use magnets to triumph over evil (and sometimes over good), and to use the magnet to follow one's own vision of true north, one's own moral compass. In the worlds of magic and mysticism, wonder and awe, there are so many tales of how to use a magnet for one's own best ends.

Wile E. Coyote spends episode after episode feeding iron filings to the Road Runner in an attempt to catch her with a giant U magnet. Instead, his magnet attracts cans of TNT, flying anvils, and the grill of an eighteen-wheeler. Before his rivalry with the Road Runner, in the early 1960s, Coyote tried to catch Bugs Bunny. Only this magnet is more complicated, an enormous magnetic contraption with an on switch and electrical sparks. He drops the Acme iron carrot into Bugs' hole and runs off home to pull out his catcher's mitt. "Lots of good minerals in this one," say Bugs, and Wile E., tiptoeing to flip on his contraption mutters, "And now he's really got a magnetic personality."

The magnet again fails Coyote. Instead of catching Bugs, his magnet draws the carrot, a mailbox, signs, cars, a boat, the Eiffel Tower, satellites, and planets, before ejecting him and his iron-conglomeration into the atmosphere. Bugs closes it out by saying, "One thing is for sure, we're the first country to get a coyote into orbit."[1]

Magneto, the magnetic super-villain of the X-Men, can control the magnetic fields of objects and planets. He has evolved over time, in the comics and or television and movies, from the owner of a magnetic ray gun (with which he could turn "paper, cloth and wood" magnetic) who had more than one origin story, now to control magnetic fields with his mind.

In the early days he fought Spiderman, and warred with other mutants who wanted to integrate into the human world, as he believed humans wanted to wipe the mutants off the Earth. As he changed over time, his backstory became that as a youth in Auschwitz, his mutant powers came on too late to save his family, but once in full force, he used them to fight humans, the humans who wish to erase mutants from the planet. Whether or not he began as a conflicted character, right versus wrong, good versus bad, in time he embraces this metaphor and his polarity seems to flip. Sometimes he fights with the X-Men and sometimes against. He reverses moral polarity, flipping back and forth to follow his own sense of right and wrong.

In many images from the early comics, Magneto levitates himself using his magnetic field. The trope of levitation has long existed with magnetics, from the early instances where gods and statues were said to levitate, from Nike on Samothrace to the Arsinoe story of Alexandria. The dual belief that one could levitate objects with magnets and the conflicting images of levitation being both godlike and demonlike weave into stories of good and evil, the polar opposites having the same qualities of attraction and repulsion.

Tony Stark, aka Iron Man, asks his assistant, Pepper Potts, to stick her hand into the metallic hole in his chest to remove a copper wire that is giving him shocks. In her fragile incompetence, she tugs the wire and pulls out the magnet that runs his heart. When she tugs it away, removing the field, he is supposed to die, but of course he cannot, being the hero. A magnetic heart may seem far-fetched to moviegoers, but it may, in the end, be true, We may find our brains and hearts produce magnetic fields, not just the electrical ones we are accustomed to, and that these fields are as critical to our being as the other functions of the human body.

The twentieth century isn't the only one with magnetic tricks up its sleeve.

In the late eighteenth century, the Mechanical Turk was a chess-playing automaton and also an elaborate hoax. Wolfgang von Kempelen built it to impress Maria Theresa of Austria and first displayed it in 1770. The Turk would sit at his chess table and play against human opponents, and win. Von Kempelon built the machine with a special compartment for a human to hide underneath. The mechanics of the chessboard required magnets to work. A strong magnet held each piece to the board, and they attracted a string from the underside, so the human chess-player could see how the Turk's opponent was moving his pieces and respond accordingly, despite being cramped in a small dark space. The design was so ingenious that the magnets pointing down couldn't be interfered with by magnets on the surface of the board. To prove this to spectators, a large magnet could be left to the side of the board, showing no interaction with the Turk's superior chess-playing abilities.

The "magnetic fantasies" described by Dunstan Lowe in his article on "suspending disbelief" are the ancient world version of these tricks. The ancients' curiosity about this stone seemed split between a desire for understanding and the question "what's in it for me."

Written reports from the ancient world told tales of statues animated by "live iron," those that floated or are magically balanced, rings that stack themselves, and a long list of saints and religious items showing such properties, though the authors describing the phenomena seem torn between God and fantasy. These tales of trickery fulfilled one purpose though, they were excellent stories, stories of the unknown and the unknowable, of the greater power of the invisible, the miraculous, which is a fine line between just that and fraud.

But what once was fraud, now is science. Or magic. It can still be hard to tell.

Most mesmerists believed they were doing good, healing and caring, but of course, not all. The showman era, vaudevillian acts, and the traveling sideshows of the style particularly found in America are chock-full of advertisements for mesmerists, magnet lifters, and other strange activities. No magnet-eaters, however, in the sideshows, though one would think that would happen. Eat magnets and then the metal sticks! You can find a handful of people on the internet who claim they are magnetic and spoons (a favorite, it seems) stick to them. Most of them have been debunked; apparently they are either rather greasy and sticky, or it is all in the camera angles, depending on who is doing the debunking. So far there is no scientific proof of the existence of (nonmetaphoric) magnetic humans.

Advertisements on the internet abound for ways in which magnets can heal, from bracelets that align one to the ley lines to a facial full of pulverized volcanic charcoal and iron, which removes impurities when a magnetic wand is used to wipe it from the face. Perhaps this is no different than adding ground magnetite to breast milk to enhance fertility, as the ancients once did. Does it work? Who knows? Today we prefer science to anecdote as our proof points, so it is unlikely we will ever know.

The world is filled with odd stories of magnets and anomalies. It is said the Earth has vile vortices, described as a "powerful eddy of pure Earth power manifested in spiral-like coagulations." Magnetic vortices are just one type we can experience. With a detailed categorization of inflow and upflow, magnetic vortices make one feel pensive due to the way the magnetism pulls into the Earth. To visit one has powerful effects on a person and their life force.

Magnetic fantasies are only one part of the tricks. Whatever tricks we humans may play, the planet may still have a few more in store for us. We know from past science that the fields have reversed, but so long ago we do not know what happens. Will birds fall from the sky? Turtles get lost?

Will all of our technology die, returning us to a new dark age? Will humans, unable to read maps or the sky, the Sun or constellations, find themselves standing about, knowledge of the world atrophied from such dependence?

Magnetic anomalies have always existed, spots where the compass does not work, unusual eddies of magnetic strength, or absence, caused by the natural world, rather than by our minds. Geoscience and physics can explain why but not how. Human minds create stories and tales to explain and describe, we envision imaginary lines—lines that are imaginary both because we cannot see them, or because we have created them to form the shape of our world. Magnetic fields versus latitude. One exists, one we created to structure the world. We bend this world to our desires, but it may bend it back, and who knows what happens then.

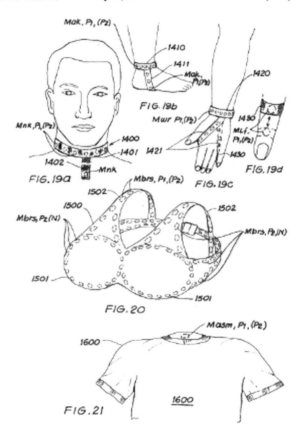

Mak, P₁, (P₂)

1410
1411
Mak, P₁(P₂)

FIG. 19b

1420

Mwr P₁,(P₂)

1430
MLf, P₁,(P₂)

1421
1430

FIG. 19d

Mnk, P₁,(P₂)

1400
1401
1402
Mnk

FIG. 19a

Mbrs, P₁,(P₂)

1502

1500

Mbrs, P₂(N)

1502

Mbrs, P₂,(N)

1501

1501

FIG. 19c

FIG. 20

Masm, P₁, (P₂)

1600

1600

FIG. 21

9 TOYS

The Ealing Studios' comedy *The Magnet* is a black-and-white film from the 1950s centered, not surprisingly, on an enormous toy magnet. The scene opens on a British schoolboy, standing on the beach in shoes, shorts, and a jacket. The boardwalk looms behind him. He looks bored as he surveys the world in front of him. He is recognizable almost immediately as a privileged child who gets his way. Something catches his eye and he pulls a handkerchief from his jacket pocket and covers his mouth before he approaches. He has a slight look of horror in his eyes, but he cannot seem to break his step. He approaches a small boy in a bathing costume in possession of a very large horseshoe magnet. The small boy is attaching it to his bucket, and picking it up, completely absorbed in what he is doing. A nanny sits off in the distance. The boy approaches, with a whiff of a bully. The younger boy looks up, sees him, and says, "I've got a magnet," and the boy replies, "Yes, and a jolly good one." Clearly, he covets the boy's toy and after a series of questions, it becomes clear he cannot simply purchase one from a nearby shop. But he wants it, and proceeds to empty his pockets, trying to swap the boy for the magnet. No luck. Not for a golf ball, not for a golf ball and a "very rare" potato, not for a tiny pistol, not for a torch, nor for a lock on a chain. The uninterested youngster turns back to picking up his bucket with the magnet, and the schoolboy walks away, dejected. But then he pauses, turns back, and offers his prize possession. An "invisible watch," which he carefully opens and shows the youngster, who says, "I can't see anything." The reply: "that proves it really is invisible," and so he goes, taking off with the magnet, leaving the child with an invisible watch. The story turns dark (if one keeps watching). The ill-gotten magnet becomes an object of bad omen, and one for which the schoolboy must pay the price, and then find redemption. Lies, dishonesty, destruction, and redemption, over a toy. Not quite the same as the Merrie Melodies cartoon, where Wile E.'s magnet is a tool, more so than a toy. Which begs the question, what is a toy?

We can all think of our own childhoods, when a toy was anything that sparked imagination, games, make-believe, or adventure. Sticks and trashcan lids, refrigerator boxes, balls and dolls, blocks, trucks and wagons. Early toys, hundreds and more years ago, were often miniature versions of adult objects, often hobbled together from scraps or leftovers. They were objects to occupy hands and minds, and to raise children to the worlds they lived in. A toy doll or cooking set, a lasso or a toy gun, are part of adult life, in miniature for children.

If you are old enough, you might remember the Edmund Scientific Catalog. Begun in the period following World War II, Edmund Scientific was one of several companies that sprang up to offload war surplus. Edmund's started out selling optics equipment to amateur craftsmen and kit-makers. Magazine advertisements covered two pages, offering ant farms and chick incubators, replica dinosaurs and mighty fishing magnets. These pages were text heavy with small drawings. A set of pages from the early 1970s offers a kit to build your own nuclear power plant, "modelled on Three Mile Island." That year the headline on their ads was, "Science is too important for U.S. kids to rank last," which apparently, they did.

The U.S. wasn't the only country making magnetic toys after World War II. West German, Japanese, and Czech toys also appeared on the market. The West German ones are quirky. A skateboarding Pinocchio, a dancing couple in lederhosen and dirndl, and perhaps my favorite, kissing Scottie dogs. In the American kit, the dogs touch nose to nose, in the European kit, it is nose to bum where the magnets attract.

In the Victorian era, the rise in the interest in science and experimentation led to an increase in lectures but also attendance at experimental evenings. These were gatherings in private homes, with apparatuses for experimentation. Both ladies and men could try their hand at science, which opened up a market for amateur scientific materials, for creating one's own experiments at home. Microscopes were one of the most common tools for home exploration; others included experiments on electromagnetism and other principles of physics.

A 1908 *Scientific American* article on toys states, "He learns best who is taught unawares, and hence when a toy illustrates a scientific principle, or serves as a means of instruction, its value is more than doubled." It describes magnetic globes to inspire navigation and exploration, blowpipes to teach about magnetic poles and resistance. In the 1880s the toy articles were less overtly about education and value but included descriptions of electromagnetic bottled imps and magnetic fishes. These toys used currents to generate motion, causing the magnets to circle or bob.

But it was the birth of the baby boomer generation that created a market for new toys to raise smarter children. It was partially demographics: more children and a larger middle class, but it was also marketing. Psychologists and educational specialists appeared in the mix. Suddenly toys were marketed as educational, toys for learning, for expanding creativity, for teaching children physics, hidden inside toys, from gravity to inertia to magnetism. Parents' magazines admonished parents that they must raise their children to be intelligent and creative, and the new middle class ate this up.

Modern toys, like modern technologies, often have magnetic parts, rather than being magnetic toys. Magnets provide an easy way to attach elements that do not require too much dexterity or strength, so small hands can use them.

In the late 1940s the Walker Art Center, attentive to the shift toward educational toys, created the Magnet Master, a toy designed to allow for creativity and abstract expressionism. It was a series of geometric shapes of bright colors, with connectors and other elements made from Alnico, a magnetic material produced from aluminum, nickel, and cobalt. They claimed it was the "first basic invention in toys since the electric train," and charged $6.95 to help your child find his inner artist. The set itself had been invented by three brothers, one of whom was an architect, whose attempts to use magnets as joints for buildings had met with failure. For children's buildings, however, it worked quite well. Embracing the new era of psychologist and educationally tested "toys" for advancement and learning, their advertisements include details on how the toy was tested with children (as well as famous artists: the painter Max Weber was shown playing along with a child in one advertisement) and thus they have proof that it will deliver the goods.

Not all toys fell into the drive for education. Whimsy has always been part of the magnet, and in particular for toys. The list of vintage magnetic toys contains more fun than education. Smethport Specialty Co was an early maker of magnetic products. Wooly Willy was one of its early unexpected successes. The packaging included a bald man with a plastic cover over him, the space filled with magnetic shavings, and included a wand. With the magnetic wand one could create hair, sideburns, a bow tie, or anything one's imagination stretched to, by dragging the filings about. Invented by Jim Herzog, no five-and-dime or toy store was initially interested in buying it. As the story goes, one shop, tired of being asked to buy it, finally bought six dozen, to prove it wouldn't sell. They sold out in a matter of days, launching Wooly Willy into the world, soon to be followed by other images: cowboys in need of hats, women in need of makeup, trolls without hair or shirts, and others.

Smethport made more than two hundred magnetic toys in its heyday. One of its best sellers involved a large horseshoe magnet set, with metal figures. Acrobats, circus players, and animals were in the early sets. "Play" involved hanging the characters beneath the magnet and blowing gently upon them, to watch them spin. Like Willy, this toy expanded into new and different characters and kits.

The Whee-lo magnetic toy worked with inertia. Not made to teach science, these toys naturally brought science with them, in their properties. Billed as the "magnetic walking wheel" it involved a red plastic wheel that traveled up and down a metal track. Held together by magnets and moving by inertia, its speed could be changed by squeezing and releasing the handle to adjust the track width. (Some internet claims say it was created to cover the inventor's legal fees incurred by lying to Congress during his 1957 McCarthy anti-American trial. It is either untrue, or history wishes to erase it, but it is fun to imagine that is how it came about.)

The Magna Doodle was a magnetic drawing board, one of many made in the 1950s. Similar to the later Etch A Sketch (which was not magnetic), a stylus allowed writing on a screen. The stylus manipulated the magnetic plasma behind the screen, and when a clean screen was wanted, a slider at the edge of the board erased and reset the screen. Lacking mechanical parts, Magna Doodles were found to work well underwater and became a tool for scuba instruction and underwater work.

Magnets were often used as bit parts, to hold kits together, and in the 1970s, to create travel versions of games. Toy manufacturers marketed travel chess, checkers, and others as a solution to the boredom of the long backseat rides of summer vacation. Train couplers, magnetic blocks, metal, and the newer, fancier wood ones, such as Tegu, are now marketed not only for kids, but for creative thinking in adults.

A search for vintage toys on eBay brought up a toy sculpture kit I had forgotten about: a black square platform with hundreds of small, flat, diamond-shaped magnets that can be massaged into any shape. But there are so many interesting toys. Sneaky Snakes, where players use a magnetic wand to steal the golden snake egg without getting bitten. One of my favorites is the Strongman, a red magnet that looks like a circus strongman, with his massive muscled arms and hands the ends of the horseshoe shape that has been common since the 1800s.

Modern magnetic toys are kinetic, architectural, and far, far stronger. These magnets tend to be round. In a recreation of the sculpture set, round balls are used instead of flat diamonds. Today you can buy your kits in multiple colors. The dark side of this appears in the *Morbidity and Mortality Weekly Report*, which lists deaths due to magnet ingestion. Children who ate more than one magnet, or a magnet and a metal toy, could find themselves with bowel perforations, necrosis, and in some cases death. If the magnets have been eaten at different times, they connect across the intestines, the extra-strong magnets holding together different sections, unmovable. An X-ray will show a mass, but not what it is, so if a parent or caregiver doesn't know a child ate a magnet, the usual advice, that it will eventually pass through the body, may result in serious damage. As the *MMWR* reports, a traditional compass run close along the abdomen of the child will indicate if the mass is magnetic, and if removal is required. A detailed report from 2006 discussed nineteen cases, including number of magnets eaten, where they were sourced, and why they ate them. Many seem to pull the magnets from older siblings' toys, and my favorite in the reason's column, "I ate three magnets on a dare." Another common reason for ingestions is the magnet's perceived resemblance to candy. At the end of the report there is a recommendation: "Magnets should never be used to emulate tongue or lip piercing."

With the increase in strong magnets in toys and the concomitant increase in injury and death to children, the Consumer Products Safety Commission issued a report that stated that toy products containing small, powerful rare-Earth magnets provide unique health hazards. Their advice? First and foremost, to keep them away from small children who might ingest them, and second, to ask the toy-making industry to use weaker magnets. After a series of recalls of toy sets due to the magnetic parts, an international toy safety standard subcommittee was put together to address such hazards.

For hundreds of years a horseshoe magnet or a set of bar magnets has been the most basic of toys, and this hasn't changed. They can still be found in toy stores everywhere, along with an impressive array of magnetic toys. The shapes and textures and strengths have changed over time, but the basic function, attraction and repulsion, stays the same, and is still fun, however odd that might be.

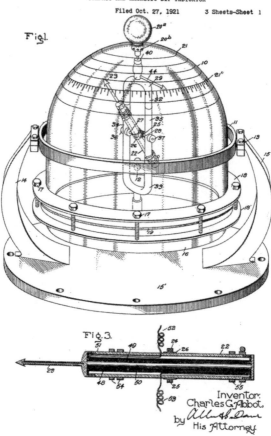

Fig.1.

Fig.3.

Inventor:
Charles G. Abbot.
by *Allen S. Dane*
His Attorney.

10 TECHNOLOGY

You may not realize it, but you are surrounded by magnets. They power all your devices, your refrigerator and microwave, your phone—landline or smart, bells and buzzers, the VCR and cassette tapes, though likely you don't have those anymore. Magnets make your phone's display work and cause the vibration. Take a spin through the hospital and you will see MRI machines, if you travel there by car, you get there with the help of magnets. They hold your loved ones to your refrigerator. Professional kitchens use magnetic times stuck to each pot, so our meals come out just right.

Natural magnets were found upon the Earth and humans devised ways to use them. We invented the compass, embedded them into communications devices such as the telegraph and then the telephone. We discovered ways to generate and store the energy from the fields, and to magnetize items with this energy. We created motors and batteries.

We created ways of seeing that extended the magical scrying of John Dee's mirrors and our ability to see the invisible, or to see into spaces previously inaccessible. The

MRI can see inside our bodies, the MEG can see the magnetic fields we produce, and the fMRI can see into our minds.

We have come a long way from small stones found on the Earth. In the twentieth century we used enormous magnets to lift and crush cars, pull items from the sea, and move objects at port and used tiny magnets to keep us connected.

War is a great driver of innovation, from the Admiralty's search for longitude to the modern era. In World War II, the Germans created technologies that had the rest of the world racing to keep up and to circumvent their skills. They created naval mines that would drop to the sea floor and align their internal compass to the spot where they stopped. A ship sailing above would pull the compass needle astray with the magnetism of the ship's body, triggering the device. An explosion would rip through the water, not blowing up the ship, but blowing it out of the water, breaking its spine when it crashed back to the sea's surface. In a rush to avoid further death and destruction, the British rigged ships to drag an electromagnet far behind on a rope, far enough that when the mine detonated it spent itself without harm. They also experimented with dragging harbors from airplanes. Later experiments found ways to pass loops of electric currents through the sea to set off a particular area, rather than having to crisscross over the entire sea floor.

In 1972 a Carrington event occurred with unexpected consequences. A few days after the event, on the fourth of August, all the magnetic mines located in the harbor in North Vietnam exploded at the same time. The idea that a massive solar flare would set off mines does not seem to have entered into the minds of the military. The government kept this classified for decades. Who knows what other magnetic secrets they are keeping from us?

Eventually researchers discovered that ships could be degaussed, removing the magnetic field from its hull so that it would not have a magnetic signature when at sea. This was done when ships were built, erasing the magnetic history of its shipbuilding location as well as the field it possessed. Later technology would use an electric coil on the ship to pass a current through the hull and make it invisible to radar.

Explorations into creating new types of magnets, super-magnets, permanent magnets, and superconductors have led to insights into how we could use magnets to see what is invisible or hidden, to change behaviors and thought, to increase computing power, and to change transportation. Each new advance in the magnet leads to advances in, well, everything else.

Early computer memory used magnetic tape to store the ones and zeros of binary code. Magnetic-core memory was the RAM for decades, notably the decades of moon exploration (1955–75). One exception was the Apollo, which used write-only core rope memory, so we did not use magnets to remember how to get to the moon and back. The moon has no magnetic field, so the rocks from the moon are entirely fieldless.

To return to TMS or stim technology, one study discovered that magnetic stimulation would reduce a subject's belief in the immorality of specific acts where the intent to harm existed, provided no harm was caused. If I coerced you to walk over a bridge I thought might collapse under your weight, as long as it did not and you survived, the subjects in the research felt this was OK. Imagine what the military or a religion could do with that technology. How do we argue the philosophical differences between right and wrong when a well-placed magnet can change their meaning?

Physicists use magnets for all manner of seeing and explaining. The Large Hadron Collider was constructed with superconducting magnets used to create magnetic fields in which experiments could be run. It contains sixteen hundred magnets, each weighing twenty-seven tons. The feat of construction alone seems overwhelming, but then came the Higgs-Boson, the "god" particle, which changed the way physicists see the world. Or perhaps we should say it exposed the way they saw the world.

Superconducting materials dramatically lose their electrical resistance when they are cooled, which allows a current to flow with virtually no energy loss. In this state of near-zero resistance they can create powerful electromagnetic fields. This could have been used to levitate the statute of Arsinoe in Alexandria, but it would take thousands of years for the advent of superconductors that could levitate objects. One of those fantasy creations is the Maglev train, short for magnetic levitation. Although James Powell invented the superconductors that made this levitation possible, he was obviously not the first to contemplate magnetic levitation.

The history of levitation of gods and saints aside, others had envisioned the idea. In 1904 Robert Goddard wrote a paper about a train that levitated, and in 1914 Emile Bachelet created a miniature Maglev train, which he displayed to dignitaries in hopes of getting funding to create the train. (At the time, electricity was prohibitively expensive for such an endeavor.) What is left of Bachelet's dream is a marvelous series of pictures of a small boy in shorts, knobby knees askew, looking slightly nauseated, riding a skeletal train about under the eyes of men in suits.

Powerful lobbies for trains and cars thwarted any attempts to develop the Maglev train in the United States. Japan has had a working prototype for decades but isn't expected to have it up and running for another decade. If they succeed, the train would travel the 286 kilometers between Tokyo and Nagoya in under forty minutes. Maglev trains can travel over 300 mph, they don't derail because they are not on rails, they can survive hurricane force winds, and they don't use fossil fuels.

Universities and DARPA are behind numerous projects exploring what's next with magnets, not only as a material, but also as a component. Yale University has built a room with the lowest magnetic field on the planet in order to isolate smaller and smaller magnetic fields, to see and study what is otherwise imperceptible when there is more magnetic noise. One study has attempted to tell the magnetic signature of the heart. Another is attempting to use nanoparticles to shift the polarity of neurons in the brain. Archaeology labs are building magnetic tools to measure the ground, the magnetic fields, and to use these fields to date materials still beneath the surface.

Seeing through solid matter. Making the visible invisible. Making the invisible visible. Going further, faster with less friction. Remembering the forgotten, communicating with the unseen. These seem to be the same, over time, of what we want our technologies to do, whether we call it magic or medicine or technology. We seem to come in circles, where what we believe and how we do it may be different, even when it still involves magnets, but the goals of humanity don't seem to change much.

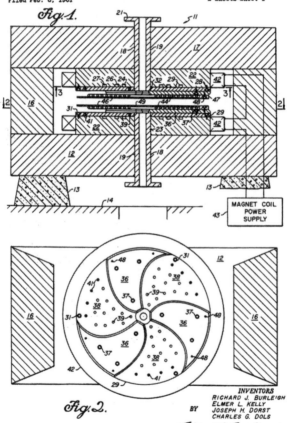

Fig. 1.

MAGNET COIL
POWER
SUPPLY

Fig. 2.

INVENTORS
RICHARD J. BURLEIGH
ELMER L. KELLY
JOSEPH H. DORST
CHARLES G. DOLS

BY

ATTORNEY

AFTERWORD

Despite its interconnectedness to our daily lives, in our devices, and in the fluctuating field that we are surrounded by, we may never think of the magnet or magnetism. Although England's Magnetic Crusade had petered off by the 1860s, research and exploration continued. And not just terrestrial observations. In the mid twentieth century, we began to explore space. The questions that had once been terrestrial now expanded into the universe itself. What's happening elsewhere in our universe? Why is there universal magnetism? Why are some planets magnetic and some not? What are these fields? How can a moon have a magnet field that is created outside the planet? With every new exploration, new questions arise. Most of these questions have yet to be answered. Even in cases where they have been answered, the answers turned out to be wrong, again and again.

In the early twenty-first century, we could suggest a second magnetic crusade was begun: for new permanent magnets, for super-strong magnets, and to understand how magnetism functions in the universe. In regard to the last, several space agencies have put satellite arrays in orbit, to track and measure different aspects of the magnetosphere and beyond. NASA's Magnetospheric Multiscale Mission has been investigating reconnection—what happens when a magnetic band snaps from one end and reconnects. What we see when this occurs is an aurora, but there is so much still unknown. The European Space Agency's SWARM array is a set of four satellites that are exploring the Van Allen belts and the South Atlantic Anomaly. They are tracking the weakening magnetic fields and find that they are weakening faster than ever recorded. This leaves the Earth vulnerable to radiation and suggests we will soon see a reversal of the polarity of the planet. But these are hypotheses based on models, we do not actually know. The geological record suggest that sometimes the fields come close to reversing, then snap back.

We still have no idea what happens when the fields reverse. Scientists have hypotheses, and grave warnings, but we won't really know the outcomes until it happens. Our planet runs on electromagnetics from our grids to our devices, from our hospitals to our homes. If it blows out for months or years, would we end up back in a dark age? Who knows? And what of all the animals who currently align to the fields? Would those creatures who migrate to known places, such as loggerhead turtles, fail to reach their traditional mating grounds? We really have no idea. All we can do is watch and wait. Unlike the hole in the ozone, it does not seem like humans are creating these anomalies and weakenings. We are just on the planet for the ride. We cannot do anything to halt this, as far as we know, but we could potentially prepare for a world in which the electrical grid is blown.

Biologists are still exploring what effects the magnetic fields have on humans and animals. They find new things—magnetic crystals in the middle ear, for instance—and different models—quantum entanglement. These are only the things we think to look for. It was thousands of years before we discovered the use of lodestones in the creation of ancient art. What else have we not thought of, imagined? There has been minimal exploration of magnetism and the sea floor, of magnetism and deep-sea creatures, and extraterrestrial exploration is still nascent. We have so much to learn.

The magnet is intricately intertwined with electricity and magnetism. To discuss one without the others is only a partial story, yet the history of electricity, its discovery and uses, is both enormous and extensively written about. While I have nodded at it occasionally, I made the purposeful decision to concern myself with more object than force, more magnet than (electro)magnetism, though that is impossible. The future of magnetism, the research going on in space and under the sea as well as in labs seeking new magnets and new ways to harness their power, is extensive. Nearly every day there is news from the scientific community on some aspect of this. For something so crucial to our existence, it continues to do a fantastic job of maintaining a low profile among most of humanity.

The more science we engage in, the stranger it gets. What started as a magical stone with descriptive properties became, with Maxwell's equations and a new vision of electromagnetism, a tearing apart of perceived reality. What we see, and the mechanical models that show us what we see, are split from the math and physics that explain what happens. Our mechanical model is not a model of the world, it is a model of how we experience the world. Faraday split these apart with his equations, in the world of classical physics. And then came the quantum.

These quantum effects that modern physics is exploring are as weird and magical and unfathomable as ancient magic. It is as real and unreal as a stone who breathes, in the daily lives of most human beings. To borrow from Plato, what was once shadows on a wall casting images of humanity, are now shadows on a wall casting images of complex mathematics. Neither really describes the "real," yet both are ways of seeing the world, with varying levels of fidelity, but not necessarily how most people experience the world. Does this matter? Probably not, because it is so complicated it is hard to know how it would change our lives if we could understand it.

What we do know is that we live in a beautiful, magical world that could in no way exist without our magnetic planet and our magnetic shields and our magnetic winds. It is impossible to understand the beauty of the geodynamo that powers our world, but we see the effects, the currents in the water, the aurora that breaks through the night sky, the ability to know where we are. Simple, complex, and mysterious.

Each year the theoretical physicists and the experimental scientists and the space explorers and the neurobiologists and the cognitive scientists (and I could go on) discover new and amazing things. I can zap my brain with magnetism and change my moral belief system and my desire for cocaine—if I zap the right spots. I can "see" how my brain works with an fMRI. Beyond the technological wonders, we are still humans, we live in a metaphorical world, we are mesmerized and seeking our true north. We desire knowledge, direction, and, perhaps, to have control taken away from us. We may never connect this to the magnet, to the extraordinary history of how humans have engaged and learned, but we still seek to make the invisible visible, to have the imaginary be real.

ESA launched SWARM. DARPA funds research to help humans use magnetism to heal themselves. Birds are found to have quantum collapsing strings to align to magnetic fields. I am certain we cannot even imagine, let alone understand how this works. We find new states for magnets such as plasma. We can finally levitate, with a little help from electricity.

Yet, what we still do most with our magnets, the reasons we care so much, is to be able to come and go, to expand and return. Much as the bands of magnetism snap off from the pole, and reattach, we as well wish to always find a way home, literal and metaphorical, and it is magnets which makes this so.

As for me, I endeavor to eat no more magnets, though sometimes I admit, I am a bit tempted to slide one into my pocket.

T. A. EDISON.
PYROMAGNETIC MOTOR.

No. 380,100.   Patented Mar. 27, 1888.

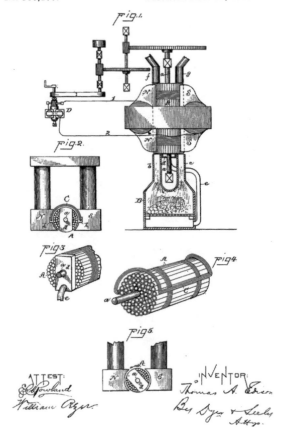

ATTEST:
E. Rowland
William Ryer

INVENTOR:
Thomas A. Edison
By Dyer & Seely
Attys.

ACKNOWLEDGMENTS

Without that first, and second, and even third set of refrigerator letters I would never have eaten enough magnets to be curious as to why all of my technology breaks, and later thus, to read endlessly about magnets, the magnetic fields of the Earth, and the history of this planetary phenomena. Without the endless curiosity instilled in me by my childhood, and the gentle suggestion that I go figure it out for myself, I might never have been caught up in this flow between magic, mythology, and science. I thank my parents for those gifts, and my friends for listening to perhaps too many stories of magnets and magnetism, most often over drinks, which I hope alleviated any pain. Particular thanks to Wayne, Siobhan, and to those who gave me old books on magnetism, homes to live in, and places to write while this came to life.

The science of magnetism is extremely complicated, and I've tried to simplify it in a way that can be both interesting and not wrong. It feels nearly impossible to be right, because the explanations are, perhaps, not useful to explaining the magic, the confusion, the endless anomalies, and the disbelief felt over the years, for each new discovery and idea. That said, the errors are all mine, and not those of the scienticsts who kindly read and assisted in my attempts to make these concepts clear, easy, and as correct as possible.

NOTES

Chapter 3

1 *Kitab al-Fawa'id fi Usul al Bahr wa al-Qawa'id* (The Book on Instructions in Rules and Principles of Navigation).

Chapter 4

1 I was once driving by a field of cows under a large set of power lines and was so intent on watching the distribution of directionality that I blew past a cop going far over the speed limit and received a startlingly large ticket. When I tried to reason with him, to explain about the cows and directionality, he seemed not only uncaring but possibly suspicious about my sanity.

Chapter 5

1 "Instructions by the commissioners," in James Clark Ross, *A Voyage of Discovery and Research in the Southern and Antarctic Regions During the Years 1839–43* (London: Murray, 1847), 1: xxii–xxvii, on xxii, xxiv.

2 From 1909 to 1912 he explored the southern realms, reaching the geographic south pole in December of 1911. These travels had given him and his crew extensive experience in Arctic and Antarctic temperatures and landscapes, and when he again looked to the north pole, this experience—from Inuit-style clothing to the use of sleds and dogs—stood him well. In 1925 he returned to the north, and in 1926 reached the north pole by airplane, the first to fly over the top of the world.

Chapter 8

1 The Soviet Union launched Yuri Gagarin into space in April of 1961, the first human to be so launched. The United States followed with Alan Shepard in May but failed to be the first. *Compressed Hare*, a Merrie Melodies' cartoon, was released on July 29, 1961, a few months after the fact.

SELECTED SOURCES

I n the spring of 2016, on a residency at the American Academy in Rome, I found myself sitting in the library in the dark of night, night after night, looking up, in every book in the Loeb Classical Library, the use of the word *magnet*. I will not cite the endlessness of antiquity, but do note that all classical references, except where noted, came from those sources. Two additional multivolume works are also worth noting, as maps to largely unseen worlds. The first is Lynn Thorndike's *A History of Magic and Experimental Science*, an eight-volume work that also contains extensive mentions of the magnet, particularly in its use for magic in Europe. Finally, Joseph Needham's work on science in China contains not only extraordinary references to the understanding of physics and geology, but many other curious things—discoveries, beliefs, and beyond, that can keep one up late at night. The other books and articles listed below were particularly interesting on their topics and will provide additional richnes than I could offer in this short book.

Bitter, Francis (1960), *Magnets: The Educations of a Physicist*, London: Heinemann.

Bray, Hiawatha (2014), *You Are Here: From the Compass to GPS, the History and Future of How We Find Ourselves*, New York: Basic Books.

Darnton, Robert (1968), *Mesmerism and the End of the Enlightenment*, Cambridge: Harvard University Press.

Heinrich, Bernd (2014), *The Homing Instinct: Meaning & Mystery in Animal Migration*, Boston: Houghton Mifflin Harcourt.

Lowe, Dunstan (2016), "Suspending Disbelief: Magnetic and Miraculous Levitation from Antiquity to the Middle Ages," *Classical Antiquity*, 35 (2): 247–78.

Needham, Joseph (1962), *Science and Civilisation in China, Volume 4: Physics and Physical Technology, Part 2, Mechanical Engineering*, Cambridge: Cambridge University Press.

Thorndike, Lynn (1923–58), *A History of Magic and Experimental Science*, 8 volumes, New York: Columbia University Press.

Turner, Gillian (2011), *North Pole, South Pole: The Epic Quest to Solve the Mystery of Earth's Magnetism*, New York: The Experiment.

INDEX

amber   4
Ampère, André-Marie   xii
Amundsen, Roald   27, 48,
   51, 52–3
"animal magnetism"   58,
   67, 69
Arab writers and navigators
   2, 7, 10, 30–1, 36
Are Frode   32
Arsinoe II   8–9, 75, 94
Augustine   62

Bachelet, Emile   95
Bacon, Francis   32
Berthelot, Marcellin   62
Bierce, Ambrose   xi
biomagnetism   35–43, 62, 101
Blavatsky, Helena   70
Booth, Felix   48
Brunhes, Bernard   24
Bruno, Giordano   20

Carrington, Richard   73
China   7, 8, 9, 10, 17, 31–2,
   57, 58, 73

Claudian of Alexandria   11
Columbus, Christopher   31
compasses   xiv, 8, 10–11,
   17–18, 22, 30–3, 36, 44,
   49, 88
Coriolis effects   22
Crookes, William   61
Curie, Marie and Pierre   xi

Daktyloi (mythical race)   9, 60
Darnton, Robert   70
DARPA (Defense Advanced
   Research Projects
   Agency)   59, 95, 103
Darwin, Charles   xi, 27
Dee, John   9, 91
Democritus   7–8
directionality   25, 35–43,
   107 n.1
Drake, Francis   18

Eddy, Mary Baker   70
Edmund Scientific Catalog
   82–3
Egypt   8–9

Einstein, Albert   xi–xii, 43
electromagnetism   61, 83–4, 100, 101, 102
Elizabeth I   9, 18
Epic of Gilgamesh   2
Epicurus   8
Esdaile, James   59, 69
Euripides   11
European Space Agency   100, 103

Faraday, Michael   xii, 102
Feng Shui   31, 32
Franklin, Benjamin   xi
Franklin, John   48

Galen   8
Galilei, Galileo   25
Gauss, Carl Friedrich   xii, 27, 50
Geodynamos   21–2, 102
Gilbert, William   18–20, 27
Gilbertus Anglicus   58
Goddard, Robert   95
GPS   xiv, 35, 36
Greece   3–4, 9–10, 11, 57, 58
Guiot de Provins   33

Halley, Edmund   22–3, 27, 50
Harrison, John   18
Hartmann, Georg   19
Hell, Maximilian   58, 67

Herzog, Jim   85
Hesiod   4
Holland, Philemon   3
Homer   2–3, 11
Humboldt, Alexander von   27, 50

Ibn Majid, Ahmad   30–1
India   57–8, 59

Kempelen, Wolfgang von   76

Large Hadron Collider   94
Larmor, Joseph   21
Lehmann, Inge   21
Levinson, Stephen   40
lodestones   3, 4, 5, 7, 9, 32, 101
Lowe, Dunstan   77
Lucretius   16

Maglev trains   94–5
Magnet, The (film)   81–2
Magnetic Crusade   xi, 51, 99
magnetic equator   45–6
magnetic fields of Earth   1, 5–7, 10, 15–27, 46–7, 62, 63, 100, 102
    biological effects, *see* biomagnetism
magnetic fields of Sun and planets   15, 22, 25–6

magnetic resonance imaging (MRI)   63–4, 71, 91–2, 103

magnetic rocks   1, 4, 6–8, 16, 24, *see also* lodestones

magnetic storms, *see* solar phenomena

magnetic temples   8–9

magnetogenetics   59

magnetoreception   7

magnets and magnetism
  animals   7, 8, 36–43, 63, 100, 103
  anomalies   xv, 17, 18, 20, 22–3, 30, 46, 79, 100
  artistic uses   5, 101
  comic book uses   75–6
  definition   xi
  divination uses   8, 9–10, 31
  eating   xii–xiv, 77, 87–8, 103
  etymology   3–4
  folk beliefs   10, 29, 62–3, 77
  hotel locks   xiv
  inclination (dip)   19, 23, 37, 42, 90
  intensity   37, 38, 42
  levitation uses   8–9, 75, 94–5, 103
  literary references   2–4, 11
  medical uses   8, 10, 57–64, 67, 78, 103
  metaphoric uses   11, 33, 103
  military uses   73–4, 92–3
  navigation uses   7, 9, 10, 12, 17, 30–3
  needles   16–17, 19–20, 30, 50
  refrigerator uses   xii–xiii, 15
  space exploration uses   42, 99–100
  technological uses   91–6, 101–3
  toys and games   28, 34, 72, 81–9
  tricks and fanciful uses   73–9

maisons magnetiques   50

mapmaking   11, 17, 46, 54–5

Marat, Jean-Paul   70

Maria Theresa   76

Marie Antoinette   69

Matthews, James Tilly   70

Matusow, Harvey Job   86

Maxwell, James Clerk   xi–xii, 102

Mechanical Turk hoax   76–7

Mercator, Gerardus   17

Mesmer, Franz Anton (and mesmerism) 58–60, 67–70, 77
Mesoamerica 6–7, 9
Morbidity and Mortality Weekly Report 87–8

Neckham, Alexander 33
Needham, Joseph 31–2
Nicander 4
Norman, Robert 19
north pole xi, 5, 19, 27, 45–9, 51–2
    magnetic north 5, 19, 45–6, 48, 50–4
    north–south axis 5, 12, 17, 37, 45
    true north metaphor 11, 33, 103
Northwest Passage 47–8, 51, 52

Olaus Magnus 17
Orphic Lithica 60

paleomagnetism 24
Paracelsus 59
Paradis, Maria Theresia von 67–8
Parry, William 51
Peary, Robert 53, 108 n.2

Peregrinus de Maricourt, Petrus 62–3
Peter of Abano 63
petroglyphs 5–6
Plato 11, 102
Pliny the Elder 3, 4, 7, 16
Plutarch 7
pole star 3, 9, 17, 32
Powell, James 94
Ptolemy II Philadelphus 8–9
Putin, Vladimir 53
Pytheas 25

quantum magnetics 43, 101, 102

Road Runner cartoons 74, 82
Ross, James Clark 27, 48–50, 51–3

Sabine, Edward 50–1
Schulten, Klaus 43
Seneca the Younger 25
Shen Gua 31
Smethport Specialty Company 85–6
solar phenomena 5, 25–6, 38, 42, 73, 93
south pole 5, 27, 45, 50, 53, 108 n.2
Space Race 74, 108 n.1

Stone of Herakles   4, 11
Strabo   16
Sucruta   58
Swedenborg, Emanuel   70

Thales of Miletus   7
Theophrastus   7
Thorndike, Lynn   62–3
transcranial magnetic
      stimulation (TMS)   61,
      93–4, 103

true north, *see* north pole
turtles   7, 8, 41–2, 78, 100

Van Allen belts   26, 100
Vikings   25, 32–3

Weber, Max   85
Wiltschko, Wolfgang and
         Roswitha   43

Zheng He   31